A GUIDE TO RAPID READING

A GUIDE TO RAPID READING
Judith Larson

Alfred A. Knopf   New York

Library of Congress Catalog Card Number: 76–129823

Manufactured in the United States of America

Composed by Graphic Techniques, Inc.,
Linden, N.J.
Printed and bound by Halliday
Lithograph Corp., West Hanover, Mass.

First Edition

9 8 7 6 5 4

Preface

The purpose of this guide is to make available the results of recent improvements in methods of increasing reading speed. The public has received some education in this area, and people are now beginning to realize that the importance and usefulness of rapid reading cannot be underestimated.

All aspects of reading can benefit from the application of principles and techniques that are covered in this guide. Those who are presently occupying a successful position in the professional or business world often feel that they cannot keep up with the vast amount of new information that is added to their field every day. This guide will provide them with tools for absorbing new information by increasing their reading speed. Furthermore, reading for enjoyment can be greatly enriched by the ability to set one's reading speed at the appropriate level, rather than being tied to one slow rate.

The results of recent studies of reading have been utilized in the development of new reading techniques. Some of the theory is presented here, though this guide is not a theoretical work that lacks practical application. On the contrary, it contains exercises, tests, and step-by-step guides for improving reading speed. The author believes that the new techniques will be better understood and utilized when the theoretical background is understood. Some effort has been made to explain to the student the underlying principles of the methods that are employed.

The course of study presented in this guide can be followed by a student who is working alone at home, or used in conjunction with supervised class instruction. The author assumes only that the person who uses this guide can read, is serious about improving his reading speed, and is willing to practice. This guide can be used by anyone who meets these qualifications, regardless of his educational level and present reading speed.

There are no gimmicks for learning to read rapidly: Much work, practice, and patience are required. The results, however, are seen early. The student will experience much satisfaction in watching his day-by-day improvement. Furthermore, the steady improvement will continue long after the course has been completed as long as the student continues to read and keeps applying the new reading techniques. New reading habits that are firmly developed now will provide lifelong satisfaction.

August 1970

J. L.

Contents

Figures

Tables and Charts

Principles on Which the Guide Is Based

1

The thesis of this book is that the reading habits of the average adult are inefficient for the task of reading. Given the requirements of the task and the abilities of the reader, the typical sequence of motor and mental acts that we call "reading" can be drastically modified in order to permit a much more rapid accomplishment of the task.

Reading habits are inefficient in the sense that a great deal of time is spent absorbing every word in the exact order in which it is printed. Although the young child must pay close attention to every word when he is first learning to read, adults can achieve a complete understanding of written material without meeting this strict criterion.

When a child learns to read he is also learning to recognize single words, to spell, to identify, and to distinguish one word from another. Recall, for example, the difficulty of distinguishing between similar words such as "then" and "than" when you were first learning to read. In addition to having difficulty with single words, the child is also unfamiliar with the structure of the language. The difference in meaning between the two sentences "Jack threw the ball hard to Archie" and "Archie threw the hard ball to Jack" is not as immediately apparent to the child as to the adult. The child cannot manipulate symbols rapidly and is easily confused by inversions in letter or word order. The adult can quickly reorganize phrases, sentences, and sequences of ideas. It is easy to see why reading habits that are first taught to the child must involve slow and orderly progress from left to right across the page, each word being taken in one at a time in the exact order in which it is printed. This process is necessary because the child possesses only a limited ability to recognize and manipulate words and word meanings. Reading habits that are acquired at this early stage of linguistic development are carried over into adulthood. Because the old reading habits "do the job," so to speak, there is rarely any effort made to change them.

The requirements of the adult for achieving full understanding of a passage are much less demanding than the requirements of a child. The adult has a vast store of experience with the language. This experience can be brought to bear on the task of understanding the meaning of words, sentences, and lengthy passages. With appropriate training and practice, the adult can develop new habits that capitalize on his familiarity with language and that permit a more rapid intake of information from the printed page. Although many adult readers have modified their reading habits over the years, either consciously or unconsciously, the reading rates that have been attained by most adults are far from the maximum possible rates. By adopting the new reading techniques described in this guide, one can increase, significantly, the speed with which written material is absorbed and under-stood.

The Basis for the Substitution of New Habits

Two aspects of the nature of reading make the successful application of rapid reading techniques possible. The first involves the characteristic of redundancy of language, and the second involves the ability of the average adult reader to integrate incoming information. In the sections that follow, each of these factors will be analyzed in some detail in order to give you an understanding of the bases for rapid reading techniques.

Redundancy of Written Material

Redundancy refers to the fact that a large percentage of the information on the printed page or in a spoken sentence is *extra* information. A sentence can be accurately understood even if some words are omitted or rearranged. Word order, in many (although, of course, not all) cases, is actually irrelevant as far as meaning is concerned. In the scrambled sentence "combed George hair his," it is evident that the correct order is, "George combed his hair." In reading this sentence, the meaning can be grasped regardless of the order in which the words occur. It is, of course, a separate problem to develop habits that will enable you to make use of this feature of the language to increase your reading speed.

There are other aspects of written material that can be relied upon to convey meaning without reading words in the exact order in which they appear. Past experience with words and language structure provide cues that will enable you to understand material without noting every word with equal clarity. You will be trained to extract the essential meaning of a passage without focusing on every bit of print. Obviously, if reading does not require that everything on the page be taken in with equal and total clarity, then reading habits that were developed to achieve this goal are inappropriate for the adult reader. Not only can the adult omit single letters from words without loss of meaning, but he can also virtually ignore entire words or phrases (for example, "Dinner is almost ready, so you ought to set the _____."). It has been estimated that over 50 percent of printed English is redundant. Full meaning can be obtained when part of the material is gone over lightly. Needless to say, the techniques that utilize these repetitive features of language must be applied with caution. Some sentences, obviously, would in fact be ambiguous if words were rearranged or omitted. The exact sequence of words may be the only means by which a particular sentence can be correctly understood: "John loves Mary" is not the same as "Mary loves John." The importance of word order is not ignored in the development of rapid reading skills, and you will be guided in avoiding the pitfall of increasing reading speed at the expense of decreasing reading comprehension. The course has been designed to increase speed while maintaining or increasing comprehension. In addition, evaluative techniques are utilized throughout the course to provide you with a check on the extent to which you are meeting these goals.

The Integration of Incoming Material

Receiving words from the printed page is the first and simplest step in reading for adult readers. The adult can store and manipulate words at a much faster rate, however, than he does in the ordinary course of reading. Motor habits for perceiving words on the printed page characteristically lead to a relatively slow intake of information. For this reason, only a small fraction of the reader's integrative ability is utilized. In this section, we will point out some of the abilities of the reader that are called into play when rapid reading techniques are used. It will become clear that these abilities are barely utilized when the typical line-by-line, left-to-right eye movement across the page constitutes the major means of taking in words.

Meaning is extracted from an array of words, a sentence, in which the individual words, the surrounding words, and the order in which the words occur are important. The array need not, however, be filled in any particular order. In effect, the mind can leave blanks and then go back to insert words that are picked up later in time. Order of input is arbitrary; it is only necessary that the reader know the *rules* of input. A sentence in German may be puzzling when translated literally, although when the reader learns the rules that govern the placement of verbs, for example, a great deal of confusion is eliminated. Similarly, if the reader himself changes the order of input of words in an English sentence, he can make mental allowances for this change. Another important aspect of the process of extracting meaning is illustrated by the following sentences which begin with the same words but have quite different meanings. "The book took John," is not a reasonable sentence, whereas, "The book took John a long time to read," is a reasonable sentence. The meaning of a string of words seems to be held in check until the array is completed. An examination of the frequency and rapidity with which these processes occur during the course of reading reveals that the human mind has a large capacity for holding information in temporary storage and reinterpreting words and phrases when new words are added to the array.

In summary, the success of rapid reading techniques is based upon the fact that order of input of words need not match the order of words on the printed page and upon the fact that the reader can reorganize and interpret words and phrases that he has already read. A vast amount of information can be taken in quite rapidly from the printed page. The reader is by no means limited to line-by-line reading in terms of his mental ability. He is, however, limited by the inefficiency of motor habits that he has been using in essentially unchanged form since childhood.

A Preview of New Reading Skills

There are two kinds of techniques that will be used to increase reading speed. The motor techniques are designed to increase the rate at which information is taken in as the eyes move across the page. The methods involve the learning of new motor skills, which are simply mechanical. The skills are applicable to fictional and nonfictional materials, and reading speeds can be adjusted to meet the demands imposed by the difficulty of the material and the goals of the reader. Another technique that is limited almost exclusively to the reading of nonfiction involves the pre-reading and organizing of material to facilitate comprehension and reduce the amount of time required for absorbing new information. The remainder of this chapter is devoted to a brief description of the ways in which the new motor skills are developed.

Most adult readers use some form of line-by-line reading. The eyes move from left to right, each word being read in the order of occurrence.

The eyes then move quickly from right to left and, simultaneously, down to the next line of print. Line-by-line reading requires a great deal of unnecessary eye movement, which, in turn, places a severe constraint on the upper limit of reading speed. All of the motor exercises that you will practice in this course are designed to eventually eliminate line-by-line reading and to substitute a much more efficient eye-movement pattern.

The basic motor skill for rapid reading is nothing more than the use of a smooth, S-shaped movement of the eyes down the page, termed the S-*pattern*, instead of the left-to-right, single-line reading that is ordinarily used. The simplicity of this description belies the complexity of the processes involved in learning new eye movements. The new movements conflict with former habits and also result in the intake of words in an unaccustomed order. Because previous reading habits are deeply ingrained and difficult to overcome, there is often a decrease in reading speed and comprehension in the initial stages of learning the S-pattern. During the early part of the course, you may become discouraged; you will almost certainly become exhausted and impatient. You will have to practice relatively dull exercises in order to lay the groundwork for complex, although efficient, reading habits in a manner similar to practicing scales when one is learning to play a musical instrument.

The elimination of former reading habits can be achieved by the gradual substitution of eye movements that approximate the final S-pattern. A series of exercises has been developed in which visual and motor movements are integrated in order to firmly establish new habits. You will first use eye-movement exercises on an inverted page with movements that are similar to your ordinary reading habits. Later, the eye movements will be quite different and will be undertaken with materials that provide the least competition from former habits. The next step in reducing left-to-right eye movement is the method of *scan-reduction*. This method involves a forced reduction in the distance over which the eyes travel in moving from left to right. With practice in scan-reduction, you will learn to make increasing use of peripheral vision and to rely less and less on focusing on every word. You will then shift to *column reading* in which words can be read with virtually no horizontal eye movement. Column reading is initiated with columns of minimal width. Then, after a satisfactory level of competence has been achieved with narrow columns, the width of the columns is gradually increased. Column reading, coupled with the method of scan-reduction, leads to the elimination of word-for-word, line-by-line reading. Next, the S-pattern, which follows naturally from a combination of column reading and scan-reduction, is introduced with columns of increasing width. By using the S-pattern, you will be able to move down the page very rapidly. Although the S-pattern produces a partial disruption of normal word order, the gradual mastering of this pattern will help maintain previous levels of reading comprehension. The reader can readily correct for the disruption in conventional word order. As was pointed out earlier, this skill is rarely called for in line-by-line reading, although it is well within the capability of the average reader. Again, repeated practice should be used to maintain high levels of comprehension when the S-pattern is introduced.

Although the pattern of eye movement is central to the development of more rapid rates of reading, the speed at which the eye travels across the page is equally important. Exercises have been developed, therefore, to increase the speed of eye movements and will be introduced at the outset. You will learn to use *hand-eye coordination* to facilitate rapid eye movement, and you will practice moving your eyes across the page at varying rates without actually reading the material. The separation of motor habits from the process of actually reading words increases the reader's awareness of eye movements and facilitates the development of precise control over reading rate. You will, eventually, be able to adjust your reading speed to different types of material in a very precise manner.

The Selection and Use of a
Practice Book

2

The techniques that you learn during the course will be applied first to the reading of a *practice book* that you will choose to accompany this textbook. Several practice books will be needed to provide practice material throughout the course. Each practice book must have certain formal characteristics that are described below and should deal with a subject that is of interest to you.

The practice book may be either fiction or nonfiction. It should not be so dull that reading is a chore, nor should it be so absorbing that you want to read it too slowly and meticulously. The best way to describe the appropriate interest level is to say that the book should keep you reading.

The level of difficulty of the practice book is an individual matter. The book selected should be quite easy for you to read and not likely to pose any problems of understanding. When you are first learning the techniques of rapid reading, it is of the utmost importance to apply the techniques to simple material. Only in this way will you be free to concentrate on the correct application of the new skills, to check your progress, and to spot mistakes in your use of each technique. Once the skills have been well established with easy material, they will be readily transferable to more difficult material. But you must attack one problem at a time. Begin using each technique on simple material, that is, your practice book, and then transfer the technique to outside reading. When first transferring the new techniques used on the practice book to more difficult material, you should not expect to read as rapidly as you do with your practice book. Your reading speed will increase, however, as you become more adept in using each technique and more confident of success.

It is absolutely essential that you select a practice book which has certain physical characteristics. The book should be printed in average or larger than average type, and the print should be dark and easily readable. There should be a reasonable amount of space between the lines (see Figure 1). Many books, both paperbacks and hardbacks, have the undesirable features of small type and too little space between the lines; therefore, a book with these characteristics should not be selected. Figure 1 shows an acceptable page setting for the practice book, and Figure 2 shows an unacceptable page setting. There should be no more than an average of ten words per line, preferably less. The importance of selecting the right kind of practice books cannot be overemphasized. Do not pick the books casually. Be sure that you have considered all of the essential characteristics in making your choice. The list of books at the end of this chapter may help you in choosing practice books that have proved satisfactory in the past. It is a good idea to provide yourself with one of these books to use as an example of the proper physical layout when you are selecting your practice books. Remember that the particular edition of the book is important. Different editions of the same book are often printed with different sizes of type, etc. When you use a book from the list given under "Practice Books," check the publisher and be sure that you have the *correct edition*.

Preparation for leisure essentially consists in the education of man in the use of his creative faculties. Man shares biological creativity with animals and it does not require learning. Creativity on the cultural level, on the other hand, can only be acquired during and after maturation. It has a cultural history, it transcends individual existence, it is molded by tradition even when it challenges tradition. This type of education enriches man's tastes and his ability to enjoy his existence beyond physical well-being; it opens up for him the unlimited frontiers of the mind.

Figure 1. Acceptable Print and Page Setting for Practice Book

SOURCE: Franz Alexander, *The Western Mind in Transition* (New York: Random House, 1960), p. 279. Used by permission of Random House, Inc.

Preparation for leisure essentially consists in the education of man in the use of his creative faculties. Man shares biological creativity with animals and it does not require learning. Creativity on the cultural level, on the other hand, can only be acquired during and after maturation. It has a cultural history, it transcends individual existence, it is molded by tradition even when it challenges tradition. This type of education enriches man's tastes and his ability to enjoy his existence beyond physical well-being; it opens up for him the unlimited frontiers of the mind.

Figure 2. Unacceptable Print and Page Setting for Practice Book

SOURCE: Franz Alexander, *The Western Mind in Transition* (New York: Random House, 1960), p. 279. Used by permission of Random House, Inc.

Written Recall: Self-Testing

The purpose of written recall is to provide you with a continual check on your reading comprehension. An individual cannot, without difficulty, estimate his level of understanding of a passage from his subjective feeling about the matter. Some people are overconfident and think that they understand a passage, although when they are questioned they can report very little of what they have read. Other people underestimate their understanding and tend to read at an unnecessarily slow rate to compensate. Upon taking the comprehension tests that are provided in the textbook or recounting a passage to someone else, you will get some idea of how well you understood a passage. As it is hardly feasible to recount your reading to another person throughout the course and as there are a limited number of comprehension tests in the textbook, it is imperative that you adopt the procedure of written recall. This procedure should be used for at least one hour every day while reading the practice book. Mark off reading passages of approximately 500 to 2,000 words in length by making a pencil mark at the beginning and end of the section. After reading the section and applying whatever techniques are being learned at the time, write down what you remember about the passage. Simply try to jot down the main ideas or events in the passage, along with any subsidiary ideas that you can recall. Complete sentences are not necessary when phrases will do, nor is correct punctuation important in written recall. Adopt the fastest method for writing your recall, using abbreviations whenever possible. Phrases and single words are more than adequate for the purpose of checking on your level of comprehension. (A sample of a satisfactory written recall is provided later in the guide at the end of the passage on the sea from James Michener's *The Bridges at Toko-ri*.)

Unless you employ the method of written recall throughout the time you are learning the techniques of rapid reading, you will be in danger of proceeding too rapidly. Students often find themselves going through periods in which their reading speed mounts very quickly, and they tend to become overconfident. At this point, there is often an increasing tendency to skim rather than read the material. The content of a passage that has just been read is only barely remembered. If you omit written recall for several consecutive days in your practice reading, you are in danger of adopting poor habits of skimming that are often difficult to break. Continual use of written recall when you are reading the practice book should help you to avoid this pitfall.

Practice Books

The size of type, spacing, and other factors in the practice books that the reader will select should fulfill the necessary conditions described in this chapter. The particular editions that are listed below are satisfactory, although the reader need not necessarily select a book from this list. As different editions of the same book are often printed in different sizes of type, the particular edition of each book listed here is important.

It is important that the typesetting of both the practice book and the books listed below be as similar as possible. If you do not choose a book from the list, compare a page in your practice book with a page in one of the books on the list. The pages should be alike in terms of size of type, amount of space between lines, number of lines per inch, and so on.

Burnford, Sheila. *The Incredible Journey.* New York: Bantam (Bantam Pathfinder Edition), 1965.

Cather, Willa. *O Pioneers!* Boston: Houghton Mifflin (Sentry Edition).

Clark, Walter van Tilburg. *The Ox-Bow Incident.* New York: Vintage Books (V-146), 1940.

Conrad, Joseph. *Lord Jim.* New York: Lancer Books (Magnum Easy Eye Books), 1968.

Dickens, Charles. *A Tale of Two Cities.* New York: Lancer Books (Magnum Easy Eye Books), 1968.

Dunbar, Flanders. *Your Child's Mind and Body.* New York: Vintage Books (V-156), 1949.

Eiseley, Loren. *The Immense Journey.* New York: Vintage Books (V-157), 1957.

Forbes, Kathryn. *Mama's Bank Account.* New York: Harcourt, Brace & World (Harvest Book, HB84), 1943.

Gardner, John W. *Self-Renewal: The Individual and the Innovative Society.* New York: Harper & Row (Harper Colophon Edition), 1965.

Grahame, Kenneth. *The Wind in the Willows.* New York: Lancer Books (Magnum Easy Eye Books), 1967.

Hemingway, Ernest. *The Old Man and the Sea.* New York: Scribner (The Scribner Library, SL 104), 1952.

Hersey, John. *Into the Valley.* New York: Bantam (A Bantam Fifty), 1966.

Hilton, James. *Goodbye Mr. Chips.* New York: Bantam (Bantam Pathfinder Edition), 1963.

Irving, Washington. *The Legend of Sleepy Hollow and Other Selections.* New York: Lancer Books (Magnum Easy Eye Books), 1968.

La Farge, Oliver. *Laughing Boy.* Boston: Houghton Mifflin (Sentry Edition), 1957.

London, Jack. *The Call of the Wild.* New York: Lancer Books (Magnum Easy Eye Books), 1967.

Nathan, Robert. *Portrait of Jenny.* New York: Popular Library Eagle Books Edition, 1962.

Paton, Alan. *Too Late the Phalarope.* New York: Scribner (The Scribner Library, SL 79), 1953.

Poe, Edgar Allan. *Poe's Tales of Mystery and Terror.* New York: Lancer Books (Magnum Easy Eye Books), 1967.

Saroyan, William. *My Name Is Aram.* New York: Dell (Laurel Edition 6205), 1966.

Schweitzer, Albert. *Memoirs of Childhood and Youth.* New York: Macmillan Paperbacks Edition, 1963.

Standen, Anthony. *Science Is a Sacred Cow.* New York: Dutton Paperback (D-16), 1950.

Steinbeck, John. *The Pearl.* New York: Bantam (Bantam Pathfinder Edition), 1963.

Subvocalization

3

Many adults have not completely eliminated the habit of making speech movements while they read. Children, when first learning to read, are encouraged to "sound out" words in order to recognize them. They are taught to pronounce each syllable of the word aloud. Upon hearing himself say a word, a child is able to identify it although the letters per se do not permit recognition. Thus, during the early stages of learning, reading is connected with overt speech movements and sounds. Although speaking while reading serves a useful function during childhood, perpetuating this habit as he grows older may severely limit a reader's potential for increasing his speed of reading. For many adults, remnants of speech movements learned during childhood reading are still detectable.

Speech movements in reading may persist into adulthood in one of three forms: mumbling, lip movement, or subvocalization. Mumbling refers to the actual reproduction of the text although in a barely recognizable form. The reader emits a steady stream of sound while reading. In lip movement, the lips form the words in the text, but no sound is emitted. Mumbling and lip movement are rarely found in adult readers. Subvocalization, however, is more common. Subvocalization refers to the almost unconscious activation of the vocal cords during reading, although no sounds or lip movements are made.

A person who mumbles, moves his lips, or subvocalizes has a limited ability to read words at a rapid rate, almost as if he had to speak each word to himself before he can understand it. As the upper limit of vocalization is approximately 250 to 300 words per minute and the average rate is considerably lower than this, speech movements will prevent the reader from achieving a rate of reading greater than 300 words per minute.

Eliminating the "Middle Step"

The intake of information while reading is analogous to the intake of information while listening. When reading, the source of information is the printed word; when listening, the source of information is the spoken word. Visual or auditory impulses are conveyed to the brain, and the reader or listener can then understand the information conveyed by the words. The reader or listener must, of course, know the meaning of the words.

Consider the input of visual information to the brain. The eye can travel over the page at a very rapid rate, and words can be transmitted to the brain at speeds much greater than 300 words per minute. The speech organs cannot, however, form words at such a rapid rate. If the reader has accustomed himself to using speech movements to form each word before moving to the next, the rate of input of the printed word to the brain cannot exceed the rate at which the reader can speak. Similarly, if the listener must write down what he hears, the rate of input of the spoken word to the brain is limited by the rate at which the listener can write. The flow of information from visual and auditory sources to the brain is outlined in Figure 3.

Activity	Source	Sensory Input	Intermediate Stage	Understanding
Reading	Printed page ⟶	Eyes ⟶	Mechanical ⟶ movements: vocal cords, lips, tongue, etc.	Brain
Listening	Spoken word ⟶	Ears ⟶	Mechanical ⟶ movements: writing	Brain

Figure 3. The Flow of Information from Visual and Auditory Sources to the Brain

If the intermediate stage (which is the mechanical movement that accompanies the intake process) can be eliminated, then intake can occur at a much more rapid rate. Clearly, a speaker can proceed at a faster rate and be well understood when the listener does not have to take notes. The mechanical stage of writing, which limits the possible rate of understanding while listening, can be eliminated, and the speaker can safely proceed at a more rapid rate. In a similar manner, if you tend to make mechanical movements while reading, elimination of these movements will allow you to read at a more rapid rate.

Diagnosis of Speech Problems

Mumbling and lip movement are easy to detect because they are accompanied by observable signs. You may simply have someone watch you as you read. You must, of course, be relaxed enough to read normally, to concentrate on reading, and to try to avoid being distracted by the fact that you are being observed.

The detection of subvocalization, however, is more difficult. You should make the following tests to determine whether or not your reading is accompanied by subvocalization. Obtain some simple reading material such as a newspaper or magazine. Then, start to murmur or whisper a string of repeating words such as, "one, two, three, four, one, two, three, four," over and over again. Or you may repeat the *first few words* of a familiar nursery rhyme such as, "Jack and Jill went up the hill, Jack and Jill went up the hill," and so on. After building up a steady and rapid rhythm repeating the words, you should then begin to read the selected sample material at your normal rate. [Continue to repeat or whisper the numbers or nursery-rhyme words as you read.] If you tend to subvocalize as you read, the murmuring of irrelevant words will interfere markedly with your reading. It may even seem to you that the printed page is blurred. You will be unable to read at your normal rate while murmuring words if you are subvocalizing. This procedure should be tried on four different selections, each being at least 300 words in length. Most people have trouble with the first selection simply because of the strangeness of the procedure, not because they subvocalize while reading. If you experience the same difficulty all four times, however, it is likely that you are subvocalizing as you read.

Cures

If you find that you engage in any speech movements while reading, it is essential that you reduce these movements before proceeding to the next chapter. The diagnostic procedure that was used above, that is, repeating irrelevant words while reading, is an effective cure for all three problems of mumbling, lip movement, and subvocalization. Begin to use this procedure while you are reading simple material at a slow rate. In fact, if you experience any difficulty in applying the technique, try fixing your gaze on one word at a time as you read and continue to repeat the irrelevant words. If you read from word to word at a slow rate, you will find that you can understand the material while murmuring irrelevant words. Your goal is, of course, to be able to read material at your ordinary rate without subvocalizing. Thus, if you can murmur or whisper irrelevant words while you are reading, you have effectively eliminated subvocalization.

The tendency to make speech movements while reading can be gradually weakened, although it is often a long and arduous task. Trying the irrelevant-word method should help you to eliminate speech movements before you move on to the motor exercises in the next chapter. Many hours of practice with this method will be substantially rewarded by enabling you to progress very rapidly in learning the new motor techniques. If you have not succeeded in completely eliminating subvocalization before you begin the next chapter, be sure to work on it *continually* while you are learning to use the new motor movements. Some students report that they seem to "hear" the words as they read them. This is another sign of subvocalization that will gradually disappear as subvocalization is eliminated.

Testing Your Reading Speed and Comprehension

4

In order to keep track of your progress during the course, keep a careful record of your speed and comprehension (S&C) scores. The speed tests and the S&C selections are provided in the textbook for this purpose. Charts 1 and 2, found at the end of the guide, are to be used for recording your scores on these selections. In addition, measure your reading speed periodically in the practice book and outside reading material. Record your progress on Chart 3.

Reading Speed

Table 1, which follows Appendix B, can be used to simplify the calculation of reading speed on selections in the textbook. All that is required is that you keep track of the amount of time that it takes to read a particular selection. Use a watch or a clock with a second hand and write down the time at which you begin to read the selection. When you finish reading the selection, again write down the time. To find out how much time you needed to read the passage, simply subtract the time at which you began reading from the time at which you finished reading. For example, you may start to read the selection entitled "Freud" at 9:34. Your finishing time is 9:38 plus fifty seconds. Subtracting the starting time from the finishing time gives a reading time of four minutes and fifty seconds for this selection. Using Table 1, read across the top until you come to the minute column headed 5, the time that is closest to your reading time for the selection. Go down the minute column under the number 5 until you come to the row that designates the particular passage that you have just read, in this case, "Freud." In the row labeled "Freud," you will find the number 212. This means that if you had taken five minutes to read this passage, you would be reading at a rate of 212 words per minute (212 WPM). Your reading rate is, however, somewhat faster than 212 WPM as you required a little less than five minutes to read the passage. If you had taken four minutes and twenty seconds to read the passage, you would use the minute column in Table 1 headed 4½ to establish your reading speed.

If you wish to determine your reading speed in the practice book or outside material, you will have to estimate the number of words read in a particular passage. It is not necessary to count every word in the passage. A suitable method is to estimate the average number of words per line and multiply this figure by the number of lines that you have read. First count the number of words in each of five lines of print in the passage that you have read. Each word counts as one word, regardless of its length. You might find that in each of five consecutive lines of print there are nine, ten, eight, ten, and eleven words, respectively. The average number of words per line is equal to the sum divided by the number of lines (48/5), or 9.6 words per line. Count the number of lines that you have read in the passage and multiply this number by 9.6 to obtain the total number of words read.

In establishing your reading speed in the practice book, however, it will not be necessary to count words per line each time. Most books use the same typesetting throughout, and a glance through your practice book will establish whether or not this is the case. The number of lines per page and the number of words per line is likely to remain constant, so that you can calculate the average number of words per page in your practice book. The calculation of the number of words in a particular passage will also be considerably simplified by using these two figures. Suppose that your practice book has 221 words per page (8.5 words per line, 26 lines per page). If the passage on which you timed yourself began in the middle of page 49 and continued to the end of page 52, you have then read three complete pages plus part of page 49. Count the number of lines that you read on page 49 and multiply this figure by 8.5, the number of words per line. Add the result to 663 (3 × 221), the total number of words on the three completely read pages, to obtain the total number of words read.

Table 2 provides a words-per-minute (WPM) chart for passages from 300 to 1,600 words in length. If, for example, it takes you two minutes and forty seconds to read a 550-word passage, your reading rate is approximately 220 WPM. This number is read at the intersection of the column headed 2½ and the row labeled 550, the numbers closest to the time and length of selection. Using Table 2 will considerably simplify your calculation of reading speed when testing yourself in the practice book or outside material. For the greatest accuracy, it is advisable to use long rather than short passages (that is, passages greater than 700 words in length) when measuring reading speed.

If you wish to calculate your reading speed on passages longer than 1,600 words, you will have to use a formula as the table does not go beyond this point. The basic formula is:

$$\frac{\text{number of words in passage read}}{\text{number of seconds taken to read}} \times 60 = \text{words per minute}$$

Divide the number of words read by the number of seconds it took you to read the passage; multiply the resulting number by 60 to obtain the number of words per minute. Suppose, for example, you read a 1,600-word selection in three minutes and twenty seconds, or a total of 200 seconds. Substituting in the formula above (1,600 words/200 seconds) × 60 = 8 × 60, or 480 words per minute.

Easy, Medium, and Difficult Material

There is no general rule for establishing the level of difficulty of written material. Some rough guidelines can, however, be used. Difficulty is often related to things that are unique to the individual: past experience, prior knowledge of the subject matter, level of interest, and motivation, to mention a few. A physicist will probably experience some difficulty reading a scholarly essay on literary criticism, just as the English professor may experience some difficulty reading an article on solid state physics. Depending upon the individual's interests and experience, reading material can be roughly categorized as *easy, medium,* and *difficult.* Your practice book should be the easiest material that you will read in connection with this guide. Newspapers, most magazines, and light fiction can be considered to be of medium difficulty. Some novels of the masters, detailed nonfiction, and technical reports, among other things, are usually classified as difficult reading.

The good reader adjusts his reading speed to meet the demands of the reading matter. When your speed reaches 1,000 WPM in your practice book, do not expect to read difficult material at the same rate. A large part of the meaning is lost by attempting to transfer the reading techniques used on easy material to difficult material in an abrupt fashion. Your speed in reading medium and difficult material will increase as you apply the new techniques to this material, although sudden changes should not be expected. Difficult material is more demanding and comprehension takes time. With continued practice, your reading speed on difficult material will increase as steadily as does your speed on easy material. Reaching the same level in terms of words per minute will take a longer time with difficult material. Remember that reading speed as such is not transferred from one type of material to another; rather, it is the new techniques that are transferred.

Comprehension Tests

Each of the S&C selections is followed by a series of questions about the passage. After you have noted the time at which you finish reading the passage, read and answer the questions. Then check your answers against the answer key. Write down the number of questions that you have answered correctly in the space provided below the last question. To obtain your comprehension score (CS), which is a percentage, multiply the number of correct answers by the number appearing to the right of the blank space. Insert your score and also record it on your progress Chart 2.

Establish your pre-course comprehension level on selections A, B, and C, which follow. Record your scores in the appropriate spaces on Chart 2. Then compute your average comprehension score on these three selections. If you obtained, for example, 60 percent, 50 percent, and 70 percent on selections A, B, and C, respectively, your average CS is (60 + 50 + 70) /3, or 60 percent. If your comprehension score is 90 percent or above on all three selections, you are reading at a speed that is below your present capabilities even without rapid reading techniques.

Throughout the course, you should have no difficulty in maintaining your average CS at a level that approximates your starting level. Although there may be temporary decreases in comprehension, you will find that the decline is rapidly eliminated as you become accustomed to each new technique. Do not slow down when you observe a decline in your CS on a few of the S&C selections. Keep up your speed, and your comprehension scores will follow. Use the rule of thumb of staying within the range of 40 percent to 80 percent, and you will proceed at a satisfactory rate. When your CS is consistently higher than 80 percent, you can safely increase your reading speed. If you score consistently lower than 40 percent (on three or more consecutive selections), you are probably applying the techniques with too much zeal.

Before learning any of the new reading techniques, you should establish your average reading speed and level of comprehension to provide a basis for comparison later in the course. You may do this using your practice book and written recall. The S&C selections that follow are also provided for this purpose.

Read Pretest A at your usual reading speed. In the space provided at the beginning of the selection, write down the time at which you begin reading. Do not read the selection either more slowly or more rapidly than you would under ordinary circumstances. When you finish Pretest A, write down the time in the space provided. Then answer the questions on the comprehension test (C Test) at the end of the selection.

The answer key for all of the S&C selections is provided in Appendix B. Score yourself on Pretest A and write in the total number correct in the space provided. Calculate your CS; determine your reading speed (WPM) on each of the pretests by referring to Table 1. The three pretests may be taken at the same sitting, or on separate occasions.

S&C Selection
Pretest A
Starting Time _____

A NUCLEAR SUBMARINE

Next morning, as is my custom when we are at sea, I took a walk through the ship, visiting every habitable area from bow to stern. I learn all sorts of things on these trips—what shape a lot of the equipment is in, what small problems have arisen or are likely to arise, and (most important of all) what frame of mind the crew is in. I know of no other way for the skipper to get the feel of his ship.

Ever since I have been going to sea in the *Skate* people have been asking me what it is really like to go to sea in a nuclear submarine. I'm always tongue-tied by this question—there is so much to say. But I think the most striking and distinct difference from any other sort of seagoing is that one is free, completely free, from the surface of the sea.

The ancient curse of the seagoer is that strangely nauseating motion imparted to ships by the surface of the sea. For centuries, sailors (especially Navy men) have denied its existence; most would rather choke than admit that it affects them. But it does. Even men who have gone to sea all their lives and have long since gotten over any trace of seasickness, no matter what the weather, know the discomfort and fatigue that come from the surface of the sea. The British have an expressive term for it: *sea-weariness*. And no one knows better what this means than those who take ordinary submarines to sea. Small and low in the water, they are miserable in rough weather and uncomfortable all the time. Forced to remain on or near the surface to get the air which their diesel engines consume in such huge quantities, they are always affected by the motion of the water.

In the *Skate*, however, we are breaking the long-established rules of sea travel. Our throbbing turbines receive

From *Surface at the Pole* by James Calvert. Copyright © 1960 by Commander James Calvert. Used with permission of McGraw-Hill Book Company.

their power from a source that has no need of oxygen or any other ingredient of the atmosphere. Traveling 300 feet below the surface day after day, we are almost devoid of any sense of motion. Only the almost imperceptible vibration of our propellers reminds us we are moving. Consequently, to walk through the ship is like passing through a small, highly concentrated, self-sufficient city built deep underground, with mechanical instruments as its only link with the outside world.

Although she is a little shorter than a conventional US diesel submarine, the *Skate* weighs—or, to use the proper naval term, displaces—almost half again as much. The difference is due to the greater hull diameter required to enclose the nuclear machinery. This, of course, allows more roomy and comfortable living conditions than those in conventional submarines. The elimination of the large storage battery and of the reserves of diesel fuel have also increased the space available for the crew.

The *Skate* is divided into two basic parts: the engineering spaces aft, and the control and living spaces forward. The extreme ends of the ship contain the torpedo tubes which are the only armament of the ship (she carries a total of twenty-two torpedoes and the tubes are always kept loaded). Each nest of tubes is serviced by a torpedo room which contains reload torpedoes and also, with characteristic economy of space, bunks and lockers for crewmen.

Almost in the exact center of the submarine is the reactor compartment. Here is located the uranium-packed atomic pile (the reactor) which provides the energy to drive the *Skate* tirelessly through the ocean depths. The reactor consists of a huge jug-shaped steel vessel, almost 20 feet high, containing a gridwork of metal-clad uranium plates. This vessel is filled with ordinary water under pressure so great that it cannot boil.

When control rods which fit into the uranium grid are pulled out to the correct positions, a controlled chain reaction of uranium fission takes place. This reaction generates heat throughout the uranium grid, which is transferred to the water surrounding it. This heated, heavily pressurized water is then circulated out of the reactor vessel, into the large cylinders of the steam generators. Here the pressurized water gives up some of its heat to another water system, at more conventional pressure, on the other side of a metal barrier. This secondary water, as it is called, turns to steam which is carried back to the engine room through heavy steel pipes. Here it spins the turbines which drive the ship and generate electric power for use on board.

The pressurized water, which is pumped in and out of the reactor every few seconds, is of course heavily radioactive. It does not, however, transmit this radioactivity to the secondary water even though it is in close contact with it in the steam generator. This is the key point in the safe operation of the power plant. The steam that goes aft to the engine room is not radioactive, and no special precautions need be taken with it. All of the radioactivity is confined to one compartment, which is safely shielded by lead plates and heavy sheets of polyethylene plastic.

Although no one can be in the compartment when the reactor is operating, this poses no obstacle to passage back and forth through the ship, as a properly shielded walkway is provided. Small round windows of heavy leaded glass are provided so that the crewmen can check conditions in the reactor from time to time.

I began my tour by walking aft through the control center and into the shielded passageway of the reactor compartment. It is necessary for me to stoop my 6 feet 2 slightly as I walk along the 30-foot passageway between the gleaming banks of stainless-steel piping. The reactor is below the floor, the only evidence of its presence a faint hum from the giant centrifugal pumps which circulate pressurized water through the grid of the reactor. The waxlike smell of warm polyethylene filled the air. I stooped to lift the metal cover from one of the inspection windows in the deck of the tunnel-like passageway. Almost 20 feet below me I could see the actual bottom of the well-lighted, deserted reactor-machinery space. All looked in good order; replacing the metal cover, I passed on into the engine room.

Passing several banks of instruments, each as large as an upright piano, I came to the two turbine-generator sets that produce electricity for this city beneath the sea. They are the heart of the ship, manufacturing not only electrical power for lighting, cooking, heating, and air purification, but also the electricity required to control the reactor and to operate the main power plant itself. If these whirring giants should fail us, the *Skate* would soon become a lifeless hulk.

C Test   A Nuclear Submarine
Finishing Time ___7.02 min___
WPM ___133___

1 Which of the following phrases best describes the subject matter of the selection?

    a. the advantages and disadvantages of using nuclear power for propulsion.

    b. the safety precautions that are taken on a nuclear submarine

    c. the physical characteristics and the mode of operation of a nuclear submarine

    d. the nature of submarine versus surface travel across the sea

2 A voyage on the *Skate* differs from a voyage on a conventional submarine in that

    a. one does not suffer from *sea-weariness* on the *Skate*.

    b. the trip is much rougher on the *Skate*.

    c. the *Skate* remains near the surface.

    d. the *Skate* is not as roomy as a conventional submarine.

3 The *Skate* carries

    a. small atomic weapons for defense.

    b. a supply of torpedoes.

    c. no defense arsenal.

    d. none of the above.

4 The atomic pile that provides energy to drive the *Skate*

    a. converts pressurized water into steam.

    b. requires water for cooling purposes.

    c. converts pressurized hydrogen into heat.

    d. produces no radioactivity.

5 The *Skate* is more comfortable than a conventional submarine because

    a. the hull is wider.

    b. storage space for the battery is eliminated.

    c. storage space for fuel is eliminated.

    d. all of the above.

CS = Total number correct __5__ × 20 = 100 %

S&C Selection
Pretest B
Starting Time _____

THE MAD DASH

Let us assume that some drug or some trick of physics could so alter a man's life-rhythm that in one second he would experience and do as much as others normally do in ten seconds. What would happen?

This man would accomplish as much in one hour as others in ten, and this one hour would seem to him like ten. The effects of the change would first of all make themselves felt in the man's conception of speed. He would be frightfully bored during every conversation because it would seem to him that his companion was taking forever to say anything. On the other hand, he would be able to make himself understood only by exercising extreme self-control; otherwise his sentences would come bursting out like rounds of machine-gun fire. He would take no pleasure in a movie because the twenty pictures that flashed on the screen every second would look like stills to him. And an automobile speeding along at 60 miles an hour would seem to be going no faster than a leisurely bicycle.

This idea is not so strange as it may sound, for nature has actually carried out such an experiment with numerous creatures. For insects who execute several hundred wing-beats in a second, man is a sluggish, slow-moving monster. A housefly, for example, would also not detect any sign of motion in "moving" pictures.

Fortunately, men's tempos are not so different from one another as we have just imagined. For even the small degrees of difference which indeed exist cause a good deal of trouble; we need only think of how trying it is for an unusually agile, fast-thinking, and quick-acting man to work with someone who is notoriously "slow on the uptake." We say of the quick and agile person that he is a "live wire." Let us call the sluggish person a "dull wire."

In a sense that is exactly what is the matter: the wires

are dull. Nerve impulses are transmitted through the body at a measurable speed. Each individual possesses his own characteristic current velocity in the nervous system. In some communication is swift, in others slow—in other words, people react at different speeds.

What does "reacting" mean? If we step on the accelerator, the automobile motor reacts; the number of its revolutions increases, and consequently so does its speed or power output. If we step on a person's foot, he reacts, cries out, draws his foot back. This reaction takes place quite fast, but nevertheless there intervenes between the stepping and the defensive reaction a whole series of important processes which in this age of great speeds cannot be disregarded.

The series begins with the reception of a stimulus by the body's specialized receivers, the sense organs. That is, we see an object, hear a sound, smell an odor, feel pressure, heat, or cold. The alerted receiver sends a rush telegram to the proper section of the brain, with which it is connected by "wires," that is, nerves. That action is the second element in the series. The brain will file away a host of less vital or trivial reports, but if the arriving impulse is vigorous enough, it crosses the threshold of sensation and sets off a chain reaction of further processes in the brain. The telegram is decoded—perception has taken place.

In the third stage of the series the report is evaluated and answered. The brain turns to the files known as "memory" to see what it is all about and what ought to be done. Then the answer is formulated and dispatched along other nerves to the various motor organs of the body, the muscles and glands. These receive the instructions and commence activity. That is the finale of the series: the reaction has taken place.

Here is a practical example from daily life. It is raining, and a fast-moving automobile approaches a street corner paved with blue basalt. There is a danger sign, and the pavement gleams in a conspicuous manner. The driver's eyes immediately telegraph to the proper department of the brain. If the man is tired or distracted, the important message remains outside the threshold of sensation, unnoticed; he "overlooks" the road sign and unsuspectingly drives on into danger. But if he is alert, the telegram arrives at its destination. The explanation comes out of the files in a hurry: Slippery road! Another department promptly adds:

Danger of skidding! Emergency! Other departments are switched in to determine what ought to be done. If the driver is sufficiently experienced, there are special orders ready and waiting in the archives: Slowly lift foot off the accelerator, make no sudden movements of the steering wheel, let the car coast down to a safer speed. Corresponding orders to dozens of muscles have counteracted the danger.

All these reactions take place in a measurable interval of time; and the driver's life may depend upon just how fast they are. Frequently a fraction of a second is crucial.

The faster we move in the realm of technology, the greater the peril from obstacles which may suddenly loom in our path. For that reason we must see and think hundreds of yards ahead.

Our eyes do in fact enable us to perceive things and events at very great distances, far greater than any of the other sense organs extend. And everyone knows, we can see much farther than we can hear or smell. All with sight we make use of the swiftest courier in the universe: light.

From a good observation post we can see a powder magazine exploding sixty miles away within one 3000th of a second. We have the impression that we have perceived the blast "immediately"—at the moment it happened. We find it hard to believe that even the light required time to reach us.

Nevertheless, light is a first-rate express messenger. If, for example, something unusual happens on the moon, which is on the average 240,000 miles distant from the earth, we see it 1¼ seconds after it occurs. If a sunspot forms upon the sun, which is approximately 93,000,000 miles distant from us, the astronomer can observe the formation after 8 minutes.

On the other hand, time begins to be squandered as soon as the light-message reaches our eyes. For our eyes are not photoelectric cells permanently directed toward a particular spot; we are constantly moving them back and forth, and these movements cost us seconds or fractions of seconds. In some circumstances we must reckon with these intervals.

Eye movements fall into three main categories. When we "peer," we make our gaze wander about from place to place in order to spy an object as soon as it appears. When we "follow" our gaze is fastened upon the object already seen. Then again, we can make our gaze jump jerkily from one point to another, for example when we read a number of miles on a dashboard, and wish to keep these within the scope of maximum visual intensity.

At high velocities such as are customary in flying, the time consumption of eye movements is of prime importance. Glance into the cockpit of a supersonic plane and you will see how many and various are the instruments, signal lights, control levers, switches, and other apparatus. How much time does the pilot need to carry out certain motions, how many seconds pass while he reads the instruments, how much precious time is lost in eye movements alone?

In order to determine the answers to these questions, specialists in aviation medicine have filmed the eyes of pilots during flight. The results are instructive: Normally, for each voluntary eye jerk in reading instruments the pilot requires from one to two tenths of a second. During a landing certain of the instruments have to be watched with particular care; for the pilot of a certain type of plane this necessity produced a characteristic triangular eye jerk lasting each time from three to four tenths of a second. In that tiny span of time a plane about to land still traverses some 65 feet.

Even without taking into account the high speeds of flight we can appreciate the importance of such investigations. For the driver of an automobile there is a similar triangular eye movement between the speedometer, the traffic signs on the edge of the highway, and the road itself. He takes his eyes off the road only for three tenths of a second each time; but if he is traveling at the rate of 60 miles an hour he will be covering some 30 feet during this moment of which he is not even conscious. Thirty feet—before he even begins to see the road again! And perception, recognition, and reaction must still follow.

Concerning Perception: The Dull Wire

The velocity with which nerve impulses are transmitted through the body was once considered the quintessence of speed. To this day we say: Quick as a thought. Technology, however, has long since outmoded the idea that thought is quick.

For the person accustomed to the modern tempo, the speed of the nerve current is disappointing: 77 yards per second, or 155 miles per hour. That is to say, the telegrams which are sent from the sense organs to the brain travel far more slowly than telegrams in telegraph wires.

Since the circuits between the receivers and the brain are relatively short, we have a false impression of the brevity of this "waste of time." If our arm were long enough for us to be able to reach out and touch the sun from our front doorstep, it would take us sixty-five years to be aware that we had burned our fingers!

While a message is on its way from a sense organ to the brain, we are unconscious of it. During this interval the perception is latent. For feeble stimuli it may take up to one third of a second before the proper department of the brain is informed; for strong stimuli the speed of the telegram is considerably increased. Red warning signals, for instance, are detected sooner than blue signals.

Physical state and aptitudes also play a part. A person suffering from fatigue requires more time for perception than someone who approaches a task refreshed and rested. People whose nerves normally have a low current velocity are the very opposite of "live wires." When an occupation calls for the mastering of difficult situations at high speeds, the candidates for it must be carefully tested, and those with slow reactions—while they may be ideally suited for other activities—excluded.

Such tests are, of course, particularly vital for the pilots of fast planes. Thousands of tests have shown that a man requires, on the average, three tenths of a second for perception. When the pilot of a Stiletto points the needlelike nose of his powerful jet plane toward the ground and goes into a power dive during which he flies three times faster than sound, he travels a distance of 1000 feet before he perceives at all. If a plane traveling at the same speed should emerge from out of a cloud, heading straight for him, neither pilot would see the other if they were less than 2000 feet apart. They would collide without having even attempted to swerve. The alarm would never reach their brains; they would not have had the slightest chance to react to the danger.

Reactions: Time Lag

After sight and perception have already consumed precious time, the most important element in the reaction series is still to come: action. When a person learning to drive takes his seat at the wheel for the first time, he has already been taught that one cannot step on the brake the very moment an obstacle appears before him on the road. He soon observes for himself that it takes time to react. Later, if something has gone amiss, he will plead "time lag" in extenuation.

The question then arises: How long a time lag is permissible? For there is no standard. One person reacts more slowly, another faster, and in critical situations the same reaction may take longer than ordinarily. Applicants for jobs which characteristically call for rapid action, such as bus drivers, airplane pilots, or rocket pilots, are therefore thoroughly tested for their reaction abilities. The faster the speeds involved, the more important these tests are. In the course of years a whole special discipline has evolved out of these studies: psychotechnics.

Psychotechnical tests are a kind of modern torture. For example, the applicant for a driver's license is placed in a simulator, an apparatus which represents an automobile, and complicated traffic situations are projected onto a screen. He is then automatically timed for the tenths of seconds which pass before he steps on the brake and jerks the wheel around. Would-be pilots are put through such tests under various artificial conditions in order to discover what effect extreme high or low temperatures, low air pressure, lack of oxygen, vibration, or loud noise have upon their ability to react.

To further the impression of systematic torture, electrocardiographs, sphygmomanometers, blood pressure recorders, and thermometers are applied to the subject to determine his "inward" reaction. Such instruments will reveal whether he is frightened, whether he is trembling, whether his pulse changes, under the pressure of various test procedures.

Most people overestimate their own ability to react. We can readily expose the folly of those who boast that they react "quick as a flash"—and possibly the quicker for a couple of beers. All we need in the way of apparatus is a smooth stick about four feet long which we mark according to a precalculated scale. We press the stick perpendicularly against the wall. The subject is then asked to hold his thumb or forefinger directly beneath and close to the stick, but without actually touching it. We are going to let the stick fall unexpectedly. He is to press it against the wall again as quickly as possible, thus bringing it to a stop. Then we read off the result; the point on the stick where his thumb rests will give his reaction time.

We can extend this instructive experiment by considering the time of day, determining the influence of practice, discovering the result of different postures, and demonstrating the effects of alcohol. People who maintain that they can drive more safely than usual after an evening of drinking will change their minds when they learn that their time lag may be "only" half a second, but that in that time their car at 60 miles an hour raced 44 feet before they were able to step on the brake pedal.

Psychotechnical tests have brought to light a number of curious phenomena. Many would-be pilots have passed the optical tests very well but failed in the equilibrium tests. Such failures rule them out as prospective fliers. Others proved extremely sensitive to acoustic stimuli. In general people react to noises faster than to images or light signals. Optical signals, on the other hand, are responded to most quickly when they are powerful and lie directly in the field of vision.

Some people can react to signals in two tenths of a second. Others, less gifted, take twice as long; some, who are especially poor, actually three times as long. Difficult and complicated tasks significantly increase reaction time. Practice cuts it down. With sufficient training, certain nerve paths are utilized more frequently; in other words, a man, like a new car, has to be "broken in." Consequently, reaction tests are followed up by reaction training. The practiced person then acts "automatically"—as, in the end, the driver of an automobile ceases to notice what movements he is making. Only when he has reached this stage does he acquire the freedom of movement and swift reactions necessary for driving in fast, heavy traffic.

Practice cuts down the reaction time for touch to 9 hundredths of a second, for noises to 12 hundredths, and for light signals to 15 hundredths of a second. These reaction times, however, apply only to very simple tasks such as releasing or pressing a switch. When the reaction requires thought, when both hands and feet must participate, it takes much longer. In these latter cases the enormous importance of practice is obvious.

An illustration drawn from the kind of traffic problems we shall be having in the near future is particularly impressive. The president of British European Airways declared early in 1955 that by the end of this century planes will be covering 3000 miles in an hour. If two supersonic planes of this type should, by unlucky chance, be flying directly toward one another, and if their pilots needed only two seconds between the first warning message from the eyes to the brain and the consequent performance of the proper series of actions, the distance between the two planes would in that brief span of time have already diminished by nearly 2 miles.

The School of Velocity

This example should make it clear that speed, though harmless in itself, can nevertheless become dangerous because the human nervous system was not created for the tempo of transportation in the twentieth century.

To be sure, we have made some adjustments in the course of the past several decades. On the streets we react faster than our great-grandfathers would have done. We feel irked when road construction forces our car to slow down and creep along. We love diversion, swift change of scene, rapid information; morning, noon, and night we reach eagerly for the latest edition of the newspaper. One hundred and fifty years ago Goethe gloomily prophesied: "I foresee a frightful age in which newspapers will appear three times a day." We live in that "frightful age" without experiencing it as unpleasant.

Restiveness, nervous haste, and lack of time have nothing to do with speed. It is not speed which makes us sick and discontented, but the mania for doing too much. Technology has presented us—and speed of transportation is an important element in this gift—with leisure time, long weekends, vacations in distant parts of the world. It is up to us to come to terms with our own weakness, which results from the discrepancy between speed and ability to react. By means of psychotechnical aptitude tests starting in early youth and repeated regularly deficiencies and weaknesses can be discovered in time and corrected by further training.

Slow reaction time is by no means man's inescapable destiny. The irresolute learn by the proper psychotechnical exercises to react swiftly; the timorous gain self-confident calm; the volatile-minded acquire the capacity for produc-

tive concentration. Thus there emerges from the psychotechnical torture chamber the modern principle of systematic
training of the nervous system. The aim is to utilize the
body's full potentialities, to open new nerve channels, form
new bridges and shortcuts.

Happy the generation to come in which not only a
privileged few but the majority of people will be able to
develop all their powers to the fullest; a generation stronger
because of technology, and complete masters of technology.

C Test   The Mad Dash
Finishing Time   _13.0_
WPM   _252_

---

1   The selection entitled "The Mad Dash" deals with

   a. the feasibility of trips to other planets.

   b. the advantages and dangers inherent in drug therapy.

   c. the speed of man's reactions to the external world.

   d. the training of jet pilots.

2   A stimulus is first picked up by the

   a. brain.

   b. nervous system.

   c. glands.

   d. sense organs.

3   Perception takes place when the

   a. brain decodes the message.

   b. message crosses the threshold of sensation.

   c. sense receptors receive the message.

   d. nervous system transmits the message.

4   Reaction takes place

   a. instantaneously.

   b. in a brief though measurable period of time.

   c. always in the same amount of time.

   d. at approximately the speed of light.

5 The swiftest courier(s) in the universe
   a. is light.
   b. is sound.
   c. are air molecules.
   d. are atoms.

6 The phrase "time lag" refers to the time it takes for the message to
   a. be decoded.
   b. be received by the brain.
   c. produce a reaction.
   d. be received by the sense organs.

7 If a sunspot forms on the sun, an astronomer can observe the formation
   a. immediately.
   b. after eight minutes.
   c. after twenty minutes.
   d. after thirty minutes.

8 Reaction time can be improved by
   a. nerve therapy.
   b. a small amount of an alcoholic stimulant.
   c. adding danger to the situation.
   d. practice.

9 Psychotechnics is the study and measurement of
   a. personality changes under stress.
   b. the validity of psychological tests.
   c. human endurance under stress.
   d. human ability to react under stress.

10 Compared to reaction time under normal conditions, reaction time after drinking alcoholic beverages is
   a. slower.
   b. the same.
   c. faster.
   d. more dependable.

CS = Total number correct _____ × 10 =   %

252wpm

S&C Selection
Pretest C
Starting Time _____

A VIEW OF THE UNITED STATES

Another barrier is the Latin Americans' persistent misconceptions of the United States. For one thing, Latin Americans have neither known nor valued their North American neighbors. On the contrary, Latin American intellectuals have always stood humbly before European culture. When they thought of themselves, it was as Europeans. If there was an indigenous note in colonial painting, architecture, and writing, it went unappreciated or was taken as evidence of a lesser competence. This attitude persisted throughout the nineteenth century. Every fashion in politics or ideas was imitated. Romanticism, positivism, Marxism, fascism, and existentialism have all had their votaries, their following, and their influence.

When Latin Americans faced the United States they saw it through European eyes, and to the Europeans all of America was inferior, whether colonial or independent. Whenever a European—Spaniard, Frenchman, or Englishman—looked at America, North and South, he saw only uncouth barbarism or at best a poor image of himself. Latin Americans accepted the European judgment because they read European and not American books and because they were educated in Europe and not in the United States. North Americans also looked at Latin America through European eyes because for a long time they too were reared on European literature and went to Europe for their "higher" education. North and South America saw each other as inferior because each in its own way identified with, and adopted, Europe's evaluation of the other America and sometimes of itself. This sense of inferiority has persisted among our southern neighbors in part because they are piqued at being left out of the mainstream of modern history. First they were dominated and enchanted by Europe and considered as something of a poor cousin. And now, quite suddenly, the United States, identified by Latin Americans as the cruder nation, has extended its arena and acts in the world as an equal to the great powers, at least in economic and military matters. Latin America feels left on the margin of world affairs. No wonder that the League of Nations, the United Nations, and other international conferences became so important. They offered a place in the sun for those who were left to live in obscurity. When a Latin American nation can be represented on the Security Council, when one of its delegates can be president of the United Nations Assembly, it has really come close to the center of world affairs. This aspiration for place, recognition, power, and influence is an honest desire held by all nations of the world. Our overwhelming power is resented because it casts a shadow over their aspiration for equality.

The hysterics of Cuban nationalism are just that. Cubans want to be independent of us spiritually—not just politically or economically. They want to carve a niche for themselves, a special place where they will not only feel secure but will shine forth to the world as a unique historic personality. That is why they are so bitter. That is why the memory of the Platt Amendment giving the United States the right to intervene in Cuba rankles so and is seemingly unforgettable. The desire to escape from our patronage and to stand out in the world as a distinctive even if little nation—like Holland, Denmark, Sweden, or Switzerland, for instance—is the inner drive. The little nations in Latin America want only to be themselves, not tied to American apron strings or led by the American hand. This is a matter about which we *will* hear much in the next generation or two. The changes forecast for the future whether violent or peaceful, whether by "revolution" or by democratic process, are part of the effort to achieve "independence"—the second liberation, as the Cubans say. And this inner passion is the greater because *this* independence cannot be won by violence. It has to be found, discovered, achieved, realized, grown into—whatever the word—so that the miracle of being at home among neighbors, without being burdened by a sense of inferiority or exalted by a feeling of superiority, comes about.

This is a matter which neither the Latin Americans nor the United States can do much about. Perhaps no one can consciously do anything about it. If we stopped feeling superior, the Latin Americans might stop feeling inferior, but that is not certain and no one can tell either of us how to begin feeling less uppish or more at ease.

The contrast between the two cultures in material possessions is so marked that there is a suspicion, if not a conviction, on the part of the Latin Americans that we want to keep what we have for ourselves and not let our southern neighbors catch up with us. When Latin Americans talk of imperialism, colonialism, and capitalist exploitation, they have in mind our growing wealth and their seemingly increasing poverty. As the gap grows wider, we are accused of deliberately making them poorer so that we can become richer. Instead of recognizing that these changes are the result of a higher rate of saving in an industrial nation and a higher rate of population growth in poor countries, that they are the consequence of the cumulative growth of a scientific technology which, by its nature, becomes increasingly diverse, specialized, and reproductive in new tools, skills, and insights, they see their inability to achieve our productive pace as proof of the exploitative nature of United States' relations with Latin America. They say: "The United States is the chief obstacle to Latin America's industrial development." As foolish as this idea may seem to those who have an average annual income of over $2,500, it is not so incongruous to our neighbors who may have to live on an annual income averaging $200 or less.

They accuse us of keeping progress away from them. In their desire to become modern, they know they must eventually reject a system which does not allow for the egalitarianism of an industrial society. But to their chagrin they find the United States supporting the status quo. Our businessmen and investors have inevitably tied their own commitments to the political world as it is. Latin Americans who accept the desirability of change are faced with the prospect of having to struggle not only against their own past but against the democratic world they hope to copy.

This is especially painful because Latin American intellectuals—more so than most in the Western world—are preoccupied with their own destiny and with their culture and its direction. This may be a heritage of the king's conscience. Just as the king was woefully aware of the mortal failings and earthly shortcomings that might keep him from glory and from heaven, so Latin American intellectuals worry about the destiny of their continent and their culture. Where they are going and whether they will achieve glory and grandeur, something unforgettable to all of mankind, is a continuing preoccupation of the most serious writers and thinkers. The fact that other peoples have managed to develop great cultures without this almost morbid awareness of self and destiny is beside the point. Their Spanish heritage provides a sense of moral purpose not only for the individual but for the whole continent. Don Quixote is still very much alive. We in the United States, who have for so long taken our destiny for granted, who allow tomorrow to worry about the next day while we live and work in the present, find ourselves portrayed by Latin Americans, who are preoccupied with the future and the ultimate, as shortsighted, materialistic, and spiritually drab. In their view of the matter, our chief concern has been immediate enrichment. As such, we could only be morally obtuse.

It is this view of the United States that helps explain certain facets of the Cuban revolution. Castro is anti-American and denounces us in hysterical terms because he not only wants to be free from American influence but because he has repudiated our claim to superiority. He asserts that the Cuban spirit is higher and richer. To be free, Cuba must, in Castro's view, repudiate not only its dependence upon the economy of the United States but totally free itself of American influence. It must be Cuban and only Cuban. This hysteria is present, real, and self-defeating. But it is part of the mood, and Latin America's early approval of Castro is largely explained by his repudiation of the United States' claim to greater virture. In this he was expressing their deepest feelings.

C Test   A View of the United States

Finishing Time _____

WPM _____

---

1 Latin Americans have generally been unappreciative of the United States' culture because

   a. they prefer their own culture to that of the United States.

   b. there is a language barrier.

    c. there is little cultural exchange.

    d. they have adopted the European point of view about the culture of the United States.

2 The power of the United States is resented by Latin Americans because

    a. their aspirations for equality among nations are so often denied.

    b. they consider the United States to be culturally unworthy of wielding great economic power.

    c. the United States acts with the great European nations as an equal, and the Latin American countries do not.

    d. of all the above.

3 In addition to producing envy, the growing contrast between the United States and Latin America in terms of material goods gives rise to the suspicion that the

    a. United States is trying to keep progress away from Latin America.

    b. United States is attempting to make Latin America into a group of colonies.

    c. United States aims to keep Latin America out of world affairs.

    d. United States' protestations of good will are a mask for imperialism.

4 Latin American intellectuals are concerned with

    a. gaining power in the government.

    b. tax reform.

    c. the destiny of their continent and culture.

    d. the philosophical implications of imperialism.

5 Castro's denunciation of the United States received support from Latin American nations because of the shared feeling that

    a. communistic forms of government will triumph.

    b. the United States is morally inferior to Cuba and the Latin American nations.

    c. Catholicism is superior to Protestantism.

    d. the material advantages of the United States will lead ultimately to world destruction.

CS = Total number correct _____ × *20* =   %

Motor Skills
Part 1: Increasing the Speed of Eye Movements

5

The first exercises are designed to break the reader of the habit of moving his eyes in discrete steps from word to word or phrase to phrase. Most adults tend to pause between words or phrases as they are reading. Reading speed can be increased with the development of smooth and continuous movements of the eyes across the page and with the development of new patterns of eye movement. In this chapter, we are concerned only with the first factor: speed of eye movement.

As discrete eye movement and frequent pausing are deeply ingrained habits, it is necessary to practice the exercises described in this chapter intensively. An alternative method, that is, simply instructing the reader to move his eyes rapidly across the page, does lead to an increase in reading rate. This increase is, however, only temporary. The reader typically reverts to slower eye movements and with good reason: The change in rate is often accompanied by a noticeable decrease in understanding of the material.

The techniques of rapid reading involve much more than an increase in speed of eye movement, but an increase in speed must precede the development of the S-pattern. It may be noted that the occurrence of a temporary decrease in comprehension has reinforced the notion that rapid reading is merely a technique of skimming. Any decrease in comprehension is, however, only temporary and is more than adequately offset by the new patterns of eye movement that are developed and by practice in organizing incoming information. Comprehension tests are provided at the end of the S&C selections throughout the textbook and must be utilized as a check on the level of understanding. Similarly, written recall must be used to accompany all reading in the practice book.

The procedures described in the next section are aimed at developing automatic, continuous, and rapid eye movements. In exercise 2, you should at first deliberately sacrifice comprehension for speed. When the eye movements are well learned, you will no longer need to make a conscious effort to move your eyes smoothly and rapidly. This goal can be achieved with no extra expenditure of energy, thereby freeing you to organize and integrate the material—and to regain and exceed your previous level of comprehension.

Speed Exercises

The exercises that follow focus on speed. Your previous reading habits will naturally make it difficult for you to adopt rapid eye movement. The use of a "crutch" has been found to be invaluable. This crutch is simply the movement of the hand across the page as a guide for the eyes to follow and is called *hand-eye coordination*.

Exercise 1. Inverted-Book Exercise. When you are first learning hand-eye coordination, avoid concentrating on the meaning of words. In order to accomplish this task, the first exercise utilizes hand-eye practice with a book that is turned *upside down*. You are thus prevented from reading and trying to understand the material when first learning to use your hand as a guide for your eyes.

With your practice book inverted, open to any page that has continuous printing, that is, no pictures or sections set in distinctive type. There should be no visual distractions on the page during this initial exercise. Starting at the top line, run your finger just under the line, moving from left to right. In other words, your finger should mimic the movement that your eyes make when reading a line of print. Unlike the focal point of the eyes, however, the finger is to move along slightly below the line. In this position, the finger will serve as a guide for the eyes to follow and as a pacesetter to speed up eye movement.

With the book inverted, simply move your finger slowly and continuously across the page, line by line, and follow this movement with your eyes. Maintain your focus at the point just above your finger and move your eyes as your finger moves. Do not make any attempt to read the words. The exercise is intended only to acquaint you with the habit of following your finger with your eyes. When your finger reaches the right-hand margin, move it back quickly across the page and down one line. There should be no delay in moving to the next line and no pausing of your finger or eyes at the right-hand margin. Pausing at this point is a common tendency that should be eliminated. Also, do not be concerned with moving your finger in an exact straight line across the page, as an approximation is sufficient for establishing hand-eye coordination.

The inverted-book exercise must be carried out at a speed that is somewhat faster than your ordinary reading speed. The main goal of the exercise is to develop an automatic following of the finger by the eyes, and at this early stage you should not be concerned with any other goal. This inverted-book exercise should be practiced for a minimum of one and a half minutes daily during the first week of the course, even after you have started to use hand-eye coordination with the book in a normal position. The habit of the finger guiding the eye must be firmly established by continual practice.

Exercise 2. Hand-Eye Coordination While Reading. The use of the finger as a pacesetter will, of course, be transferred to reading with the book in an upright position. At the outset, when hand-eye coordination is attempted while reading, there may be some disruption of the smooth coordination that has been established with the inverted-book exercise. This disruption is attributable to a natural tendency to slow down when you come across unfamiliar words or when you are uncertain about the flow of ideas in a sentence. For the establishment of hand-eye coordination, *pausing must be eliminated even at the expense of a decrease in comprehension.* Move your finger rapidly across the lines, with your eyes following your finger. Read and try to understand the material as well as you can. Remember, however, that your primary goal is speed. You should not resort to pausing, slowing down, or rereading a line, but keep up a steady and continuous movement of the eyes across the page. The continuous use of hand-eye coordination should be maintained during a one-hour daily practice session.

In addition to eliminating pausing, you should move your finger along at a speed that is uncomfortably fast for reading. In effect, your eyes should race over the lines. It is not unusual to begin hand-eye coordination at a rate twice as fast as your normal reading rate. If you find this difficult, be certain that you are moving at least *uncomfortably* fast, that is, at a speed that noticeably exceeds your normal reading speed. *Force yourself to continue at this rapid pace.* Do not be concerned with your level of understanding of the material. Naturally, you should try to understand as much as possible. But do not slow down or pause in order to gain fuller understanding. Above all, do not go back over a line which you have already read. Using this procedure, you will, of course, miss some of the meaning. This is to be expected and will be more than offset at later stages. Remember that the goal at this point is solely to develop a particular high-speed eye movement and an automatic following of the finger by the eyes.

The use of hand-eye coordination will enable you to eliminate any tendency to go back over parts of a line that you have already read. Eye-movement studies have shown that readers occasionally reread a word or a phrase. Yet there is substantial evidence to show that comprehension of a passage is not reduced when readers force themselves to continue in a forward direction across each line. The hand-eye technique is invaluable in helping to eliminate undesirable habits such as rereading. Any retrogressive movements are brought sharply to the attention of the reader. When the focal point of the gaze wanders away from the finger, a danger signal is provided. The hand-eye method is also indispensable in setting the pace for materials of different difficulty and in marking the pattern for the eyes to follow (Chapters 6 and 7).

Double Reading

In addition to reading a passage at high speed the first time, the only way to develop facility with the techniques of rapid reading is to practice each technique while you are *rereading* a passage at a stepped-up pace. As you have already read the passage once, you will be able to "let go," on your second reading. Regular practice with rereading is essential for the acquisition of rapid reading skills. It is not sufficient to practice the motor techniques without learning to apply them at a rapid rate. If you have any reluctance in moving quickly across the page, this reluctance must be overcome. The method of double reading has proved to be a successful solution to the problem. The skills that you learn while rereading a passage will eventually be applied almost automatically to your subsequent first readings of new material and you will notice a gradual transfer of movements that you use on "forced speed" second readings to your first readings.

Steps for double reading

Begin by reading a passage in your practice book that will take you about two minutes to read. Decide on the length of the passage according to your most recent score on a test of reading speed. Before you start reading, mark the section in your practice book and note the time at which you begin reading. Read the passage, record the time it takes you to read it, and write your recall. Now, reread the same passage from beginning to end forcing yourself to increase your reading speed. Complete the passage in approximately one and a half minutes, that is, speed up enough to cover the material in about thirty seconds less time than it took you for the first reading. After you have had some experience with double reading, you will be able to estimate fairly accurately the amount of speed-up that will be required on the second reading to reduce the reading time by approximately thirty seconds. When you complete the second reading, add any new ideas to your written recall.

When you begin each practice session outside of class, the entire procedure of double reading with written recall should be applied to three to six passages, each taking you approximately two minutes to read the first time. Reduce your time to one and a half minutes on the second reading of each of these passages. Next, use somewhat longer passages and apply the double-reading technique. For example, you might read a passage that takes three minutes on the first reading and try to reduce the time to two and a half or two and a quarter minutes on the second reading.

From now on, all of your reading in the practice book is to be done with the double-reading technique. Practice outside of class for one hour each day. At each practice session, begin with double readings of relatively short passages and then increase to longer passages. Do not, however, use the double-reading technique on passages that take you more than five minutes to complete on the first reading.

When first learning hand-eye coordination, many people find it difficult to force their eyes to read over the lines at a speed that is much greater than the speed at which they normally read. Yet this stepped-up pace of reading is a necessary stage in learning the new motor skills. If you find yourself unable to overcome a reluctance to speed up, resign yourself to reading the same selection over and over again until you become very familiar with that selection. Use the hand-eye technique each time you read the selection. The selection will become easier and easier to read through at a rapid rate. Repeat this procedure with a number of different selections, and you will find that rapid eye movement with hand-eye coordination is feasible. You will begin to read new passages more rapidly than before. Always use written recall to evaluate your comprehension. Many students tend to overestimate the extent to which they have missed the meaning of a passage—written recall will help to correct this impression. At the same time, slight decreases in comprehension are quite natural; continued practice will enable you to raise your comprehension to a high level.

To establish hand-eye coordination as a strong habit, use it in your outside reading as well as in your practice reading. The only difference will be in the speed at which you read outside material. Of course, it is not feasible for you to read outside material twice or to read it as rapidly as you do the practice material. Nevertheless, you should transfer each of the new motor skills to all of your reading, even though you do not use the stepped-up pace that you use with your practice book. The more you employ the motor movements on different types of material, the more adept you will become at using them. Gradually, you will find yourself reading outside material more rapidly even when you are not making a deliberate effort to do so.

The hand-eye method will be used throughout this course. Use the method in *all* of your reading from now on. Accustom yourself to following your finger with your eyes. Be sure that this habit is automatic and reliable before you proceed to the next stage of the course.

S&C Selection

Starting Time _____

SPELMAN COLLEGE

Spelman College in Atlanta revealed, in the years of sit-ins and strife, this conflict between old and new inside the Negro world. At Spelman, there was always an emphasis on manners and morals, in the narrow sense. The Spelman girl was for generations the recipient of well-meant advice from her teacher-elders: be nice, be well-mannered and lady-like, don't speak loudly, and don't get into trouble. Spelman was pious and sedate, encrusted with the traditions of gentility and moderation. But with the sit-in movement, there began a revolt of Spelman students against these exhortations, against tradition itself.

Not that Spelman girls stopped being "nice"—they stopped being genteel only long enough to walk back and forth in front of two Atlanta supermarkets, with picket signs demanding an end to discrimination against Negroes. They were still well-mannered, but with this went their adherence to the declaration that they would use every method short of violence to end segregation. As for staying out of trouble, they were doing well until that March 15, 1960, when the great sit-in took place. Of the seventy-seven students arrested, fourteen were Spelman girls. The staid New England women missionaries who helped found Spelman College back in the 1880's would probably have been surprised at this turn of events, and conservatives in administration and faculty were rather upset. It looked at that moment as if respectability were no longer respectable among young Negro college women.

"You can always tell a Spelman girl"—alumnae and friends of the college had said for years. The "Spelman girl" walked gracefully, spoke properly, went to church every Sunday, poured tea elegantly, and in general had all the attributes one associates with the finishing school. If intellect, talent, and social consciousness happened to develop also, they were, to an alarming extent, by-products.

With the sit-ins, this began to change. It would have been an exaggeration to say, in the spring of 1960: "You can always tell a Spelman girl—she's under arrest." Yet the statement had a measure of truth.

Not only did Spelman girls participate strongly in all the major actions undertaken by students of the Atlanta University Center; they added a few touches of their own. White Atlantans, long proud that their "nice" Negro college girls were staying "in their place," took startled notice of the change. When a Spelman girl riding downtown on the bus took a seat up front, the bus driver muttered something unpleasant, and a white woman sitting nearby waved her hand and said: "Oh, she's prob'ly goin' downtown to start another one o' them demonstrations."

Even before the sit-ins, the reputedly sweet and gentle girls began to cause trouble. As early as January of 1957 they were challenging segregation. That year they aroused the somnolent legislators of the Georgia General Assembly into a near-panic by attempting to sit in the white section of the gallery. When the speaker of the house saw the young Negro women with one white and one Negro faculty member sitting in the "white" section, he seemed to develop a quick case of apoplexy and rushed to the microphone to shout: "You nigras move over to where you belong! We got segregation in the state of Georgia!"

Attendants hurried upstairs to enforce the order. The group quietly rose and, after a brief consultation, decided to watch the proceedings from the "colored" section, having already demonstrated their real desire. The presence of the white teacher (myself) with them in the "colored" section created much nervousness in the chamber below; the legislators, forgetting about the business at hand (a bill on trout fishing), craned their necks and stared. Not quite sure whether the teacher was a dark white man or a light colored man, they hesitated to order him out.

A footnote on the ironies of Southern courtesy must be added here. When the group was sitting, to the satisfaction of the speaker of the House, in the "right" section, he dispatched a messenger to find out who they were. Then, the information in his hand, he came to the microphone again and announced, as was apparently the custom with all visiting groups: "We hereby cordially welcome the students and faculty of Spelman College to this session of the General Assembly."

When the next session of the legislature convened in early 1958, Spelman students in the Social Science Club decided to pay another visit. Not ready yet, as they would be two years later, to go to jail, they decided to protest silently by standing in the white section. Again, the House speaker dashed for the microphone, grabbed it from a legislative orator, and demanded that the group leave. The students filed out through the nearest door, to the accompaniment of loud applause from the legislators, who saw this as a military victory. But the applause had hardly died down when the group reentered the gallery through another door and stood near the colored section, maintaining their resolve not to sit down in a segregated section.

It took several more attempts during subsequent legislative sessions, a march downtown, a dramatic picket line circling the gold-domed State Capitol in the spring of 1961, and the election of a Negro Senator to the legislature, to accomplish the desegregation of the gallery. When that day finally came in January 1963, Spelman students were in the gallery to mark the occasion, watching with an interest both personal and social as Leroy Johnson, a Negro lawyer, placed his hand on the Bible to take his oath of office. Three white Senators put their hands on the same Bible at the same time, an act that might be considered revolutionary were we not living in an age where the impossible takes place daily.

Also before the sit-ins and before bus segregation was declared illegal, some Spelman girls rode in the front, withstanding the glares and threats of fellow passengers and the abuse of bus drivers. Once, a white man pulled a knife from his pocket and waved it at one of my students sitting opposite him in a front seat. She continued to sit there until she came to her stop, then got off. Spelman students spent hours between classes at the county courthouse, urging Negroes to register for voting. They made a survey of the Atlanta airport for a suit to desegregate the airport restaurant, and a Spelman student took the witness stand at the trial to help win the case.

Such activities brought some bewilderment to the conservative matriarchy which has played a dominant role in the college's history. The twelve-foot-high stone wall, barbed wire fence, and magnolia trees that encircle the Spelman campus have always formed a kind of chastity belt around the student body, not only confining young women to a semi-cloistered life in order to uphold the prevailing conception of Christian morality, but "protecting" students from contact with the cruel outside world of segregation.

A similar barrier, more spiritual than physical, surrounded the entire Atlanta University Center, where interracial faculty, occasional white students, and frequent white visitors created a microcosm of the future. In the Center, racial barriers were gone and one got a feeling sometimes that this was not part of the Deep South. But for many years, that insulation which protected the University Center's island of integration also kept the city of Atlanta from feeling the resentment of Negro students against segregation. It was a comforting protection, but it also helped perpetuate the mystique by preventing contact. Thus, Spelman girls, more sheltered than women at other colleges and now the first to leave the island, began to cause little flurries of alarm, not only in the segregated world outside but in the sanctuary itself.

C Test   Spelman College
Finishing Time _____
WPM _____

---

1 Spelman College was known for generations for its

    a. emphasis on manners and morals.

    b. radicalism.

    c. pacifism.

    d. emphasis on political activities.

2 Alumni of the college took pride in the Spelman girls'

    a. political interests.

    b. propriety and social graces.

    c. intellectual accomplishments.

    d. grounding in the arts and sciences.

3 Spelman girls were

    a. not known for their respectability.

    b. politically conservative.

    c. actively involved in the demands to end segregation.

    d. not involved in the sit-ins.

4 Spelman girls started to challenge segregation as early as 1957 by

    a. using public water fountains that were labeled "White Only."

    b. using public restrooms that were labeled "White Only."

    c. picketing the Georgia legislature.

    d. sitting in the section of the Georgia legislature that was labeled "White Only."

5 The result of the Spelman girls' activity was to

    a. further isolate Negro college girls from the white community.

    b. accomplish desegregation of the gallery in the legislature.

    c. injure the academic reputation of Spelman College.

    d. enhance the academic reputation of Spelman College.

CS = *Total number correct* _____ × *20* =   %

S&C Selection
Starting Time _____

TRAINING A DOG

"Training a dog" has a number of different meanings. A working dog is trained to do a job; protect people and property, tend livestock, pull a cart or sled, track down and apprehend wrongdoers, act as sentries or even combatants in war, help police control riots or potentially riotous situations. A hunting dog is trained to track down and point or flush game birds and to retrieve them after they've been shot, or to nose out and follow the trail of four-footed game— rabbits, foxes, deer, bears, and even lions. A pet dog is trained to have manners, to use the outdoors rather than the indoors as his bathroom, not to get on those pieces of furniture which are forbidden to him, not to pester the family or guests for tidbits at mealtimes, and to observe certain rules formulated for the protection of his own life. There is also training for obedience tests or shows, but while some elements of this training are useful, the mere *spectacle* of obedience I find distasteful.

Most working dogs have an instinct for doing the job for which they're intended. A sheep or cattle dog will take over the care of a flock or herd almost from puppyhood. He is usually given a bit of training by people, but more often he is taught the tricks of his trade by his mother or some other older dog.

A bird dog, too, is born with an instinct for his trade. Even a puppy pointer, setter or spaniel will frequently come to a point the first time his nose comes in contact with the scent of game, but invariably his youthful exuberance will cause him to raise the game before the hunter is ready. He must be taught patience and restraint. A bird dog also needs to be trained not to chase other animals, principally rabbits, an enticing sport but a grievous fault. The classic punishment for this dereliction is to shoot the rabbit, tie its carcass around the dog's neck, and force him to carry it for several hours. The humiliation is so excruciating that one treatment usually breaks the dog forever of rabbit-chasing.

Hounds require little or no training. Scenting, tracking and hunting game are born in them, and they love the sport of it all. Some of the big, raw-boned hounds are courageous fighters and will corner and badger the biggest, toughest animals until the hunter has a chance to catch up with the chase and dispatch the quarry. Professional lion hunters use this kind of dog but they also always include a couple of Airedales in the pack. Not a few hunters owe their lives to the fact that an Airedale will always go for a lion, or tiger, or any other animal which is closing in on his man. It frequently means the death of the Airedale, but this does not deter him.

Rather strangely, a pet dog needs more training than a working or hunting dog. Living in a house, and abiding by the somewhat peculiar customs and manners of man, does not come naturally to him. Whether or not he thinks it all a bit on the silly side has never been determined, but he learns to go along with it, usually quickly and effortlessly.

To me, there's one fundamental rule in training a pet; *reward but do not punish.* If you observe this rule, you will soon see that the withholding of the reward will in itself be punishment enough.

This gentle philosophy of training is by no means universally accepted. Some people feel that "spare the rod" spoils the dog, as well as the child. They go for discipline rather than compliance or coöperation, and they're ready to use sternness of voice and attitude, and even physical measures ranging from whacks with loosely rolled newspapers to genuine beatings with sticks or straps. People in this group almost always stop short of cruelty, mix reward and gentleness with their sternness, and end up by both giving and receiving affection.

There is a third group which goes further to insist on complete *mastery* of the dog, on immediate, almost craven, obedience. This is the school of training known as the German School, used mostly with German shepherds and Dobermans, and almost certainly the reason why these two splendid breeds have suffered a reputation for viciousness and treachery. The keystone of this school is cruelty. The result, naturally, is viciousness and a distrust, even a hatred, of humans.

Most trainers dislike to use the choke collar, and when they do, use it gently. Devotees of the German Method consider this a ridiculous display of softness. When they use the choke at all, they use it with considerable force. But they prefer their own collar with sharp spikes on the inside, so that if the dog pulls he is punished by sharp pains, even broken skin. The classic way to break a dog of jumping up on people is to step on his hind feet when he jumps. Most trainers dislike this, too, but do it the few times necessary to break the dog of the misdemeanor. They make it a point to wear light sneakers and step gently on the dog's feet, not hard enough to bring forth even a faint whimper. The German Method will have none of this effeteness. A German Method trainer puts on the heaviest, thickest-soled shoes he owns and slams down on the dog's sensitive toes. He believes in instilling in the dog the fear of God, he the trainer being God. He shouts his orders in the voice and tone of a Nazi Gauleiter and demands instant and uncompromising obedience. Anything less is punished by hard slaps in the face, or whippings with a whip, a rope, or even a heavy chain. He gets his obedience; and he can have it.

For many years, the Doberman was the proudest achievement of the German method. The Doberman was a dog specially bred by a German dog catcher named Fritz Doberman as the "perfect watchdog." Viciousness and ill-temper were bred into him, and sustained in him over the year by German Method trainers. He was the "perfect watchdog" all right; the only trouble was he sometimes had difficulty distinguishing between friend and culprit, and lacerated or even demolished the person he was supposed to protect. Shelley Berman has a gruesome, but funny, line: "The Doberman is a great dog; you raise him from a puppy, and when he's eight years old he kills you." It's not quite that bad, but neither is it altogether Mr. Berman's raffish imagination. For many years I have read or had clipped for me any story about dogs in newspapers or magazines. If the story didn't tell the breed of the dog involved, I'd try to get it from the publication or the wire service. When it was a story about a dog turning on, and maiming or killing, a member or friend of his own family, it would almost always turn out to be a Doberman, or, less frequently, a German shepherd. In fairness, it must be said that the German shepherd also stood out prominently in the stories of dog heroes.

About twenty years ago, a change came into the life and character of the Doberman. A dog fancier named Len Carey bred and lovingly raised a Doberman named Ranch Storm Dobe. He was a great family pet but he was also started on a show career. He was a sensation. He finally appeared in Madison Square Garden, at the Westminster Show, and won Best in Show at that most glittering of all dog shows. He went back to his beloved family, and to the business of siring. The following year, Len Carey made the courageous decision to have him defend his title in the Garden. The chances of his repeating were, say, about 1,000,000 to 1. But he made it! Storm was not only a great champion, and a great dog in intelligence and disposition; he was a great breeder of champions and of great dogs in intelligence and disposition. There's hardly a good specimen of the breed today that isn't able to trace Storm Dobe in its ancestry. He, and his great and good friend, Len Carey, performed something of a miracle for the whole Doberman breed. But still, please, don't go up to a strange Doberman and embrace him.

C Test   Training a Dog
Finishing Time _____
WPM _____

1   Professional lion hunters include Airedales in the pack because

   a. Airedales have the best sense of smell.
   b. Airedales are intelligent.
   c. an Airedale always attempts to protect his man.
   d. Airedales give loud warning barks.

2   The author believes that the best way to train a pet is to use

   a. the German method.
   b. reward only.
   c. punishment only.
   d. a combination of reward and punishment.

3 The German method is based upon complete mastery of the dog. This is established by

    a. developing trust and affection in the animal.

    b. never punishing the animal for mistakes.

    c. the use of extreme cruelty and physical punishment.

    d. the use of immediate rewards.

4 The German method was used to train the Doberman as a watchdog. The one drawback was that the dogs sometimes

    a. attacked friend and foe alike.

    b. were afraid to attack.

    c. gave excessively loud barks.

    d. were easily won over by strangers.

5 Which of the following is *not* characteristic of the German method

    a. use of a spiked collar.

    b. giving commands in a low voice.

    c. demanding immediate obedience.

    d. instilling fear in the animal.

6 The effect of the German method is to develop

    a. excellent show dogs.

    b. perfect watchdogs.

    c. dogs that display loyalty and love of the master.

    d. dogs that display viciousness and distrust of humans.

7 The Doberman

    a. cannot be mastered except by the German method.

    b. has a vicious temperament.

    c. can be a good family pet.

    d. never attacks humans.

CS = Total number correct _____ × *14.3 =*   %

THE SAUNA

The history of the Finnish steam bath, or *sauna*, goes back well over a thousand years and possibly more. It is even believed that the sauna was where Vikings took their ease, and was what they dreamed of when on raiding expeditions far from home. While the Halls of Valhalla waited in the great beyond for the slain heroes of battle, the saunas with their comforts and delights waited the return of the living. To them its magic never failed and no doubt they played a role in imparting its joys to other peoples. The Mandan Indians of the western plains were using such baths when explorers first found them, and it is thought by some that they may have been influenced by blond Norsemen who penetrated the continent before Columbus.

Its use is ancient, possibly discovered first by prehistoric men who basked in the live steam coming from some volcanic fumarole. Whatever its origin, the principle is the same everywhere, vapor generated by throwing cold water on heated stones. There are as many variations in method and ritual as the people who have learned to enjoy it. In Finland, however, it reached its highest refinement, became so closely allied with tradition and culture that it is inconceivable to think of this hardy race without it.

According to early records, saunas were originally only excavations in the earth, built into the sides of hills, and served both as baths and family dwellings. Later, they were cabins built on flat land with a living room attached; finally, saunas became separate buildings near the water.

In the sauna's mellow, cozy warmth, many a tale was told and many a song sung during the long blank winter nights of the north. It was here the legends of *Kalevala* were told and handed down from generation to generation.

The sauna was considered a protection from all troubles, physical as well as of the mind, and it is not without reason the Finnish people say, "If spirits, a sauna, and tar do not effect a cure, then a disease is fatal." In the days of the dark past when demons and spirits were abroad, the Mistress of Pohjala cast an evil spell on all people, bringing pestilence, until it was feared all must die. Vänämöinen, the ancient bard and seer, healed them with the sauna and his incantations. Ever since, the steam bath has been held in reverence and to this day no one within its sacred walls must speak or think of evil.

All over the north of Europe, in the Baltic States as well as in Scandinavia and Finland, the sauna is spoken of with affection and delight. Its use has been so closely woven into the fabric of these cultures, it can never be forgotten even by the most sophisticated. Finnish emigrants brought the custom to America as early as 1683—and it was said that a settler built his bath house first, then his house and barn. In America today, as in Finland, every Finnish farm has its sauna; even in towns and cities one finds them built into homes, or, if this is impossible, into public baths, so important has it become to the way of life of these people. Some are elaborate now, have lost their simplicity in chrome and steel and glass, but the spirit lives on and still invokes its magic, bringing rest and peace to weary bodies and souls.

My sauna cabin is primitive, one step removed from the first excavations in the hillsides of Finland. I wanted it that way for I felt it must be close to the earth, so much a part of the natural environment that simple values would not be lost. Nestled in a grove of cedars back of the beach, its logs are hand-hewn, carefully notched, and weathered a silver gray. The cabin is small, only ten by ten, but a stoop faces the bay which gives it depth and view. In the old days the roof would have had a hole for the smoke to escape, but now a stove pipe leads through it. Handmade benches are around three sides, and there are wooden pegs for towels and clothes. A window is under the peak of the roof and another looks into the birches. Beyond this there is nothing. Simplicity is the keynote, but when steam rises from the stones and the sprays of cedar give off their fragrance, the sauna comes into its own.

Tall aspen stand among the cedars surrounding the cabin, and as the wind blows they whisper an ancient song. Along the ridge protecting it from the north, are birches growing among the rocks, clusters of striped maple, and hazel. Chickadees and nuthatches are around my sauna cabin, and in one of the tallest trees, pileated woodpeckers have built their nest.

A flying squirrel lives in a hole under the roof and, when it comes out, it spreads its legs and sails to the nearest balsam. I saw it the other night and its eyes were liquid and black, its fur a greyish tan and softer than chinchilla, its wing strips edged with sable. A beautiful creature, I am glad it has taken its abode in so important a place as my sauna.

Along the trail to the lake are huge stones with depressions between them reaching down to the dark, wet roots of the cedar. The boulders are covered with sphagnum and in it grow gold thread, violets, and strange fantastic fungi. All these living things are part of the sauna cabin, as they are part of the woods and rocks around it. It is a place of delight and beauty woven into the experience itself.

In the old tradition and as a mark of hospitality, it is the custom to invite a guest to partake of a sauna with you, but only if the guest is willing and deserves the honor. So when my son came home after several years in Libya and Lebanon and full of the things he had seen and done, there was no question of what to do first. It was an afternoon in September that we started the fire in the barrel stove. The water was cold, the ash trees along the shore were turning yellow, the maples beginning to flame. Only the finest spruce was to be burned that day, for this was a great event for us both. Two cedar switches were prepared. We picked them carefully, only the softest and finest from the lower branches of a tree that grew close to the water. The cabin was swept and clean, and a hand-woven rag rug of many colors was laid out smoothly for our feet. Buckets were filled from the lake, two placed on the rocks above the stove, two on the bench before it.

As preparation, we spent several hours at the woodpile, hauling logs of birch, aspen, spruce, sawing them into proper lengths, splitting them to size, and piling them neatly. While we labored with axe and saw, the smoke curled high above us, the rocks became hotter and hotter until they hissed and spat when water was sprinkled on them.

Toward evening all was in readiness. We opened the door and the bathhouse smelled as it should, rich with the pungence of burning, the odors of hot logs and of many saunas of the past. We stripped and took our places on the lower bench.

A dipperful of water tossed onto the rocks all but exploded, instantly filling the cabin with steam. Then more water, again and again, until the steam began to penetrate our bodies. When we had become accustomed to the heat, we moved to the upper bench where it was more intense. As we sat there, we became one with the rising vapors and the crackling spruce in the stove.

"Dip your cedar switch," I said, "dip it in your bucket and sprinkle the stones."

Bob did so, and the air was full of fragrance.

"Hold it to your face," I told him, "hold it close and breathe deeply."

The oil of cedar went into the passageways of our lungs, scoured and renovated them until they were clean and fresh. The moist warmth caressed us and filled us with a lassitude that dispelled all thoughts, and had we not been faithful to the ritual, we might have been tempted to stay and miss one of the greatest thrills of the sauna, the exhilarating plunge into the cold waters of the lake. Watching Bob, and knowing myself, I felt we could wait no longer. The time had come.

"Let's go," I said.

Heated through and through, we dashed down the trail, splashed into the bay, swam furiously for a moment, then returned. How good to feel the warm steam again, and now the perspiration literally rolled off our bodies until we shone and gleamed in the firelight.

"The stones," Bob asked, "where did they come from?"

"The old gravel pit," I answered, "the big ones are on the bottom, smaller ones on top. Notice they are all smooth and dark and of a size, small enough to give maximum surface but not so small they'll cool."

"Polished in some glacial river," he said "and now they're here where they belong."

"Turn your back," I ordered, and I whipped him with the cedar switch until his skin was red and covered with the flat green tips of the branch ends.

He did the same for me and we laughed with the good feeling that was ours of cleanliness, of warmth and blended smells. No ordinary bath could equal this. The pores themselves were cleaned, the blood brought into circulation by the plunge, the entire system recharged, stimulated, and relaxed.

"This is it," said Bob, "elemental; we need nothing more. I had forgotten how good a sauna really could be."

He held the cedar against his face, breathed deeply once more.

"The smell of cedar," I reminded him, "is an incense that carries thoughts to heaven, which is why all worries leave."

"And all evil," he replied, "all intrigue and ambition."

I threw on another dipperful. White steam surrounded us and swirled along the ridgepole.

"About ready," announced Bob, and once more we ran to the beach, this time swam far out for the water was like silk to us, and we did not feel the cold, were conscious only of floating without effort and drifting in a medium as warm as our own bodies.

We went back to a third and last steaming and, when we returned to the lake for a final dip, the sun was tinting the water, the west was pink and blue, with a broad band of color in the bay. We swam through it and then into the band, lay there in its iridescence, looking toward the sauna in the cedars. Smoke still rose from the chimney, though the fire was almost gone, and we could even smell it there on the water.

After we had cooled, we swam to the beach, went up the trail again, opened the door and windows wide, and dried ourselves leisurely. It was almost dark now and we sat on the lower bench before the open door of the stove and toasted our feet in the glow of the coals. The hot steam was gone and the cool night air felt good to us. The coffee pot was hot and we took it outside, sat on the stoop and drank cup after cup.

"Mead of the Vikings," said Bob.

The horizon was a dull glow against the dark of the ridges. A sudden breeze fluttered the aspen leaves far above, and we could hear the soft rushing of the river at the outlet a mile away. Loons called time and again, first the wild laughing calls, then a last long mournful note.

There was nothing of great moment to talk about, but within us was a feeling of well-being in which the affairs of the world seemed far away and unimportant. Ours was a sense of fullness and belonging to a past of simple ways. After a time we went in and dressed by the firelight. Before going up to the big cabin for supper we stood outside for a while. A sliver of a new moon hung low in the southwest and we could see the outline of the old. Far out on the lake, I heard a flock of mallards. Not long now and great Vs of them would be winging toward the south. Stars were beginning to show and Venus hung like a great lamp in the darkening sky.

This was the time of magic when the world was still, this the feel of dawns and of awakenings at night, of hush and quiet. Life was simple and complete.

Finishing Time _____
WPM _____

Motor Skills
Part 2: Reducing the Amount of Horizontal Eye Movement

6

The ability to see things beyond the focal point of vision is called peripheral vision. Words on a page can be accurately perceived even if the reader does not focus on every single word. Movement of the eyes to the end of each line is not necessary for comprehension of the entire line. Peripheral vision is effective under a wide range of conditions. It is obvious, for example, that while you are staring at a particular object in a room, you can still see other things to the right and left of that object. Similarly, when you look at something at close range you can see many things to either side and behind the object. Peripheral vision enables you to see things in vertical as well as horizontal directions.

You can demonstrate peripheral vision with the following procedure. Hold your hands in a vertical position approximately twelve inches in front of your eyes, with palms facing you. Look directly at the palm of your right hand and fix your gaze on it. Then slowly move your left hand to the left, away from your right hand. Hold your right hand stationary in front of you, maintaining your focus on it. Move your left hand to the side very slowly until you reach the point at which your left palm disappears from your view. You will have to move your left hand quite a distance away from the right hand before you reach this point. Now, reverse the process and focus on your left palm placed directly in front of you. Move your right hand away slowly until you reach the point at which your right palm disappears from view. As you will notice, both palms can be seen when they are quite far apart, even though your eyes remain focused on only one hand. Similarly, words in a line of print can be perceived even though you do not focus directly on every word. Despite this fact, most readers tend to move their eyes all the way to the end of each line and to begin a new line by focusing on the first word in the line. The exercise of *scan-reduction* is designed to weaken and eventually eliminate this habit. It is true that words at the extreme periphery of vision cannot be accurately perceived. The method of scan-reduction must be applied with cognizance of this fact.

Exercise 3. Scan-Reduction. In your practice book, draw vertical lines down the right and left sides of the page, approximately one-half inch in from each margin. The placement of the lines is shown in Figure 4. Later on, the actual drawing of lines will be unnecessary. For the present, the lines are used as guides for the distance over which your eyes will travel as you are reading. Instead of focusing on every word from the beginning to the end of a line, begin by focusing at the vertical line on the left side of the page. Place your finger at this point. Move your eyes across the line using your finger as a guide and move to the next line as soon as you reach the vertical line on the right side of the page. Read down the page in this fashion, always using your finger as a guide. You will find that comprehension is not reduced by using this method, and speed is increased. Use scan-reduction in your practice reading and on the selections at the end of the chapter. After a while, you need not actually draw in the lines; instead, imagine that they are there and reduce your scan as before.

From now on, employ the scan-reduction technique on everything that you read. Move your finger to the next line of print *before* you get to the end of the line that you are reading. Continue to use the aid of drawn-in lines on the page even after you feel that scan-reduction is occurring fairly automatically. This is not a difficult habit to develop. Most students will be satisfied with their ability to employ scan-reduction after a total of fifteen to twenty pages of reading with drawn-in lines as guides. Note that practice with the scan-reduction method is to be spread out over a period of a week to ten days. You cannot learn the habit in one or two practice sessions and expect to maintain it for a long period of time. Therefore, scan-reduction while reading with guidelines must be practiced over and over again. In your daily exercises for the next week, include five minutes of practice in scan-reduction with drawn lines. In addition, employ scan-reduction (with imaginary lines) in all of your reading.

This book is devoted to diagnosis and not to treatment. How the higher faculties of man can and should be cultivated, encouraged and developed is the province of public education. Education for creativity, however, can only flourish in a society which has grown out of its present, almost exclusive preoccupation with material standards of living. It can only be hoped that western humanity will not need the further spread of juvenile delinquency and neurosis, cold and hot wars, to be awakened from its present torpor and to be convinced of the sterility of its current ideals.

Figure 4. Scan-reduction lines

SOURCE: Franz Alexander, *The Western Mind in Transition* (New York: Random House, 1960), p. 278. Reprinted by permission of Random House, Inc.

Exercise 4. Column Reading. *Column reading* is a second technique for establishing habits that minimize left-to-right eye movement across the page. Materials for the exercises are provided on pages 67–90. Words are printed in columns of varying width, beginning with one or two words per line. You will practice reading these columns without left-to-right eye movements. The development of the final technique of rapid reading, the S-pattern of eye movement, must be approached gradually. Column reading is one of the important steps along the way.

Read the following column of words by running your finger and eyes down the line drawn through the middle of the column:

The
army
and
the
navy
were
at
odds
concerning
the
best
method
for
obtaining
supplies

You may notice that even with this very narrow column of words, you have a tendency to move your eyes to the left each time you moved down to the next line. A column of one-word width, such as the one you just read, can be read easily without any horizontal eye movement. The habit of left-to-right reading persists even when unnecessary. It is now your task to establish the habit of moving your eyes only in a vertical direction when practicing the column readings. Begin to reach this goal by paying special attention to the focal point of your eyes. When reading the columns, focus at a point just above the tip of your finger. As you run your finger down the center of the column, keep your gaze fixed above your finger. Use a slow movement down the page for the first few column readings and concentrate on keeping your eyes focused at the center of the column.

A line is drawn through the center of the columns on pages 65–69. Follow the line with your finger and eyes as you read the column. Make every effort to eliminate left-to-right eye movements. Read each column several times. When you feel satisfied that you have minimized left-to-right eye movements, try to increase your speed. Additional columns of one-word width are provided for practice.

The exercise of column reading is extended to wider columns on pages 73–90. Do not hurry through these exercises. Instead, spread your practice on column reading over a full two weeks by practicing for a short time every day. Read the same columns over and over again. Becoming familiar with the content of the material will enable you to pick up speed comfortably in moving down the column. A good rule is to force yourself to move rapidly down a column and then to read the column again immediately at the same rapid rate. Several rapid readings of a column are preferable to a few slow readings for building up good vertical eye movement. Use these columns repeatedly for practice of this movement.

As you progress to wider columns, you may find that using the entire hand as a guide for the eyes is preferable to using one finger. Some readers tend to read only the middle words in the column when they use one finger as a guide. Try substitution of the hand as a guide with columns of four or more words in width. Make an effort to read the entire line with a *minimum* of horizontal eye movement.

With diligent practice, the reading of columns that are provided in the textbook will enhance your ability to read an ordinary page of print with a minimum of horizontal eye movement. It is clear, however, that vertical eye movement alone is not sufficient for the reading of most material. The printed page is generally wide enough to prevent the reader from taking in the entire line in one glance. Some amount of left-to-right movement will be required.

The S-pattern, introduced in the next chapter, depends upon the integration of all of the habits learned so far. The previous habits must be firmly established before the S-pattern is attempted.   Only in this way can you ensure the development of correct eye movements and long-lasting retention of these habits.   The final technique of rapid reading is the S-pattern.   Using this pattern, horizontal as well as vertical eye movements are made simultaneously.   The extent of each movement is adjusted by the reader to fit the type of material being read.   Size of print and type of material will be used to monitor the sweep of the hand and eyes as they move down the page in the S-pattern.

On	sauntered	you
our	over	use,
way	to	Granny?"
to	a	I
the	barefooted	asked.
Great	old	The
Smokies,	woman	old
my	in	woman
wife	a	took
and	faded	the
I	cotton	pipe
stopped	dress	from
to	who	her
look	sat	mouth
at	rocking	and
a	on	smiled.
particularly	the	"Truth
colorful	porch,	is
display	corncob	son,
of	pipe	I
hooked	in	don't
rugs	mouth.	ever
at	"What	smoke.
a	kind	I'm
roadside	of	just
cabin.	tobacco	providin'
I	do	local
		color."

From "Life in These United States" by Irving S. Quale, in the *Reader's Digest* (February 1949). Reprinted with permission from *The Reader's Digest*.

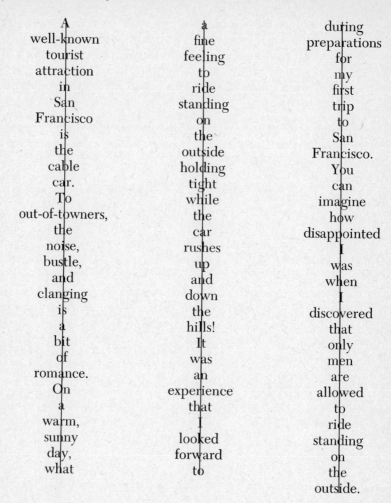

A well-known tourist attraction in San Francisco is the cable car. To out-of-towners, the noise, bustle, and clanging is a bit of romance. On a warm, sunny day, what a fine feeling to ride standing on the outside holding tight while the car rushes up and down the hills! It was an experience that I looked forward to during preparations for my first trip to San Francisco. You can imagine how disappointed I was when I discovered that only men are allowed to ride standing on the outside.

motor skills part 2: reducing the amount of horizontal eye movement

A
group
of
Navy
men
being
tested
on
aircraft
recognition
complained
that
it
wasn't
humanly
possible
to
recognize
the
planes,
for
the
pictures
were
flashed
on
the
screen
for
only
1/50

second.
But
the
officer
giving
the
test
insisted
that
this
was
time
enough.
To
prove
it,
he
said
that
he
would
show
a
slide
for
1/500
second,
and
for
them
to

write
down
what
they
saw.
The
slide
was
flashed,
and
the
whole
group
burst
into
laughter.
They
all
had
time
to
recognize
that
it
was
a
picture
of
a
shapely
nude!

From "Humor in Uniform" by Robert F. H. Ritch, in *The Reader's Digest* (March 1954). Reprinted with permission from *The Reader's Digest*.

Lyndon Johnson, complaining that Republicans were on both sides of a budget argument, told the Senate they reminded him of an unemployed Texas schoolteacher who applied to a hill-country school board. "We would like to retain your services," they told him, "but tell us this: There is some difference of opinion in our community about geography, and we want to know which side you are on. Do you teach that the world is round, or do you teach that the world is flat?" And the applicant, Johnson went on, immediately replied: "I teach it either way."

Daniel Defoe, the author of *Robinson Crusoe,* was once condemned to the stocks for political reasons. The London mob was so vicious that people were often stoned to death in the stocks. Defoe wrote a humorous poem in which he tried to persuade the mob not to attack him. The mob was so delighted with the poem that they threw flowers instead of stones.

72

a guide to rapid reading

It
is
not
probable
that
man
for
long
will
remain
satisfied
only
with
the
comfort
afforded
by
technology.
He
will
build,
as
he
always
did
in
the
past,
on
this
abundant
economic
foundation
second
and
third
stories
of
civilization
on
the
symbolic
level.
Eventually
he
will
again
seek
new
expressions
for
his
creative
mind,
in
new
art,
in
scientific
curiosity
for
its
own
sake,
in
basic
research,
in
playful
exercise
of
his
potentialities
beyond
the
immediate
needs
of
survival,
in
the
art
of
living
which
goes
beyond
material
standards.

There are many places where people have lived long enough to have sunk their roots deeply, who somehow have absorbed the character of the country they have chosen. I know parts of New England where the people are as native as the partridge in their upland pastures, places in the South where people have the feel of whippoorwills and mockingbirds and magnolias in their blood, and in the West where mountain ranges and purple vistas are a part of their lives. Wherever you go, you will find them, but most always away from the arterials and big towns, in the back country, where they are still living close to the land. Theirs is a certain contentment with things as they are, a perspective that comes only with living in one place a long time, and a loyalty to the old ways that fights change and modernization.

Two English schoolboys took a dislike to each other, and the hatred grew more intense as the years passed. One entered the Royal Navy and finally became an admiral; the other went into the Church and eventually was made a bishop. Years later they met on a London railroad station platform. They had changed, of course, and the bishop had grown very plump, but they recognized each other. The bishop swept up to the admiral, who was resplendent in his uniform with medals and gold braid glittering all over him, and said: "Stationmaster, from which platform does the 10:05 train leave for Oxford?" The admiral promptly retaliated: "Platform 5, madam. But in your condition, should you be traveling?"

From "Laughter, the Best Medicine," in *The Reader's Digest* (October 1955). Reprinted with permission of United Press International.

A person who has lived during the past fifty years of rapid cultural change, who in his early years has experienced the last phases of a more individualistic and creative era, and who later has been exposed to the advent of the statistical man, will naturally look back nostalgically to the good old days. He is likely to react to this change as to something destructive; he is likely to evaluate the present trend as dehumanization, a degeneration of those values he absorbed as integral parts of his self, the governing principles of his behavior. Only after detached reflection will he be ready to question the universal validity of this reaction.

The usual throng of noisy tourists was watching the annual Corn Dance at a pueblo near Sante Fe, when a group of strangely garbed Indians approached the dancing area. The women were dressed in violently colored slacks and floppy hats; the men wore loud sports shirts; all were equipped with sunglasses and carried cameras. Closing in on the dancers, they stared, giggled, talked loudly and pointed boorishly; they got in the dancers' way taking pictures. Then they pulled up boxes, sat down, opened paper bags and began to eat sandwiches, strewing wrappers carelessly on the ground. When they withdrew, a shamed and respectful crowd of white tourists watched the rest of the dance in silence.

From "Life in These United States" by John H. Burma, in *The Reader's Digest* (March 1949).
Reprinted with permission from *The Reader's Digest*.

Man has become an extension of the machine, which no longer serves him; he has become its slave. Moreover, automation reduces working hours, creates leisure which man is not able to utilize in any creative fashion. Initiative and fantasy wither away; a bland stereotyped personality who does not aspire to form his own destiny emerges, who does not want to be different, to be himself, since none of his individual characteristics are needed or encouraged. All this is but the adaptation of the personality to the existing socio-economic structure. The plasticity of human nature seems to be immense; it appears possible that such a gradual transformation of personality structure can be accomplished without provoking internal revolt. A new species, the mass man, is in the making.

The study of
personality development
as well as
history points to
two fundamental
trends in human
behavior: on the
one hand, to
adapt, and on
the other, to
grow and create.
Adaptation seeks
stability and security,
the preservation of
the status quo.
Growth and
creativity seek
change, bringing
into being something
not there before.
Man is a
restless animal who
is not satisfied
by adapting himself
to his environment.
He succeeded
spectacularly in
changing his
environment by
creating civilization;
instead of adapting
himself to nature,
he adapted nature
not only to
his needs but
to his fantasy.
As long as
this basic human
trait—creativity—
not only on
the biological but
also on the
symbolic (cultural)
level persists—in
other words, as
long as man
remains human—
the merely security-
seeking conforming mass
man is not
likely to stay
here forever.

From *The Western Mind in Transition* by Franz Alexander. Copyright © 1960 by Franz Alexander. Reprinted by permission of Random House, Inc.

A college professor
was to give
a final examination
to the students
in his course
entitled "Communication."
The college was
undergoing a period
of renovation, and
there had been
many problems with
classroom assignments
during the year.
Since the examination
was scheduled to
be held in
a part of
the campus
with which he
was unfamiliar,
the professor arrived
fifteen minutes
early in order
to locate
the room.
He was disturbed
to find that
the building
was locked.
After hastily
searching for a
telephone, the
professor called
the custodians and
explained his problem.
The custodians
promised to take
care of the
problem immediately.
After twenty minutes,
when no custodian
had arrived, the
students were
getting restless.
As it was
a warm day,
the professor
suggested that
the students sit
on the lawn
and write
their examinations.
Five minutes
after they had
settled themselves and
started writing, there
were sudden
cascades of water:
the lawn
sprinklers had
been turned on!
The students
finally relocated
themselves and the
examination continued.
The professor
announced that his
next semester's class
would be canceled
so that he
could do research
on the communications
problem with the
custodial staff.

After living
all my life
in the country,
I decided to
take a new
job which
meant a move
to a large,
distant city.
A sense of
newness pervaded
my life,
and I decided
some mental
stocktaking was
in order.
It seemed to me
that a good
way to take
advantage of
the sense of
renewal was
to get rid
of some
unpleasant habits.
I decided to
stop smoking.
After much struggle,
I finally gave
it up.
One of the
things that helped

was my disgust
at the way
cigarette smoke
masked the fresh
country smells.
After settling
in the city,
I went out
for a long walk.
It was very
new and exciting
to be walking
down a city
street instead of
across country fields.
Soon, though,
my eyes
were smarting
and the air
had a
gritty feel.
The smell of
exhaust fumes
was overpowering.
I realized that
in spite of
all my struggles
I was
"smoking" again—
not cigarettes,
but city air!

In the midst
of preparing luncheon
for her bridge
club, my elderly
neighbor was
interrupted by a
salesman of packaged
food mixes. She
was telling him
in no uncertain
terms that she
was too busy
to be bothered
when there was
a screech of
brakes outside, then
screams. In the
middle of the
street lay her
little granddaughter.
In the ensuing
turmoil, Grandma
forgot her luncheon,
the cake in
the oven and
the salesman until
assured at the
hospital that
the child was
unhurt except for
bruises. She hurried
home, expecting
to find everything
burned to a
crisp and the
house robbed.

Instead, her guests
were playing bridge
and beside each
lady was a
little pile of
packages. On the
kitchen table stood
the cake, expertly
frosted; luncheon was
ready to be
served. On another
pile of packages
was this note:
"I took the
cake from
the oven
when it was
done. It is
topped with one
of our special
frosting mixes. I
learned to cook
in the Army,
so think you'll
find everything
satisfactory. Your
bridge club is
convinced that food
mixes are the
coming thing. They
bought liberally after
my demonstration. Am
leaving some packages
for you too.
Will collect tomorrow."

From "Life in These United States" by Lillian Howland, in *The Reader's Digest* (December 1948).
Reprinted with permission from *The Reader's Digest*.

This starts right at
the beginning. It seems
a dog and a
cat lived with Adam,
and they drew up
an agreement stating
that the dog would
do all the work
outside the home and
the cat would do
the work inside. And
the cat was to
take care of the
agreement itself because
she could find
a safe place
inside to keep it.
After a while, the
Devil—up to mischief
as usual—put the
notion into the dog's
head to be
discontented with his
bargain. So one day
the dog said to
the cat, "Why should
I have to stay
outdoors, sun, rain or
cold, and bark at
thieves and take care
of the whole house,
while you sit safe
by the fire—purring!"
"Well," said the
cat, "an agreement
is an agreement."

"So it is, so
it is," said the
dog. "But suppose we
see that agreement,
which was put in
your care—perhaps it's
time to reconsider it."
So the cat went
to get it from
its hiding place in
the attic and discovered
that the mice had
nibbled it to pieces
and lined their nests
with the pieces.
The cat was furious
and chased and killed
as many mice
as she could
(so that's how
that one began).
When she came out,
the dog said,
"Where's the agreement?"
and of course, she
didn't have it, so
he went for her.
Today the first thing
a dog always says
to a cat is,
"Where's that agreement?"
And when the cat
cannot produce it, he
goes for her and
chances are he chases
her up a tree.

People in the know
tell us never to
leave your car unlocked
because this makes life
easy for car thieves.
But in very hot
summer weather, rolling
up the windows and
letting the car sit
locked up tight in
the boiling sun
can do all
sorts of damage.
The concentration of
heat inside a
closed car can
dry out lubricants
in instruments. It can
melt radio components
and has been known
to deteriorate safety glass
. . . even to melt and
fuse rubber seals.
Another thing such
heat can do
is dry out
upholstery stitching until
it pops—particularly
in vinyl upholstery.
The answer is to
lock your car and
try to park it
in the shade. But
if you can't, keep

one window open slightly—
just enough to let
air circulate. What
about rain pouring in?
Better a little water
than deterioration from
heat. Besides you can
protect your upholstery
by using a water
repellent spray made
for this purpose.
Ask your service station
man to clean the
inside of your car
with his vacuum which
is more powerful than
yours and designed for
cars. While you
are there, buy
some upholstery cleaning
preparations and a can
of protective spray.
If your service station
doesn't stock these
things, your auto supply
store will. It
is important to do
the job with the
right cleaning agents
and not with
just any detergent
or cleaner you
have on hand.

American individualism asserted itself,
in the main, on the
economic level. The nation was
until recently absorbed in the
application and further development of
modern technology for the conquest
of a vast wilderness.
This preoccupation with technology and
economic advancement became the
most powerful organizing
principle also within the personality.
The basic existential dilemma—
"What is the purpose and
sense of existence?"—did
not become a pressing issue
for a nation which had
a vital and concrete answer:
to build a technically efficient
world with a steadily rising
material standard of living for
everyone. Such a concrete and
timely goal appropriate to the
life situation of the population
did not leave room for
idle contemplation about the meaning
of existence. Every able-bodied
and able-minded person could
freely participate in the pursuit
of highly practical goals and
find full outlet in
advancing his individual economic interests.
The problem of finding new
emotional outlets and new
inspirations has become an
issue only recently, with the
advancing organization of big
industry and big business, which
has reduced the opportunities for
exciting individual ventures, has favored
conformity and routine, and has
at the same time secured
comfortable economic standards for
the majority of people.

For the majority, individualistic
aspirations are no longer
realizable in the arena of
action and can be satisfied
only by watching western films
and criminal dramas or
by participating passively in
sports events as spectators.

To complete the survey of
the primates, we should say
something about a curious, rare
little creature called the tarsier
which lives in the
East Indies. It is of
great interest to zoologists
because it is the only
survivor of a kind of
primate common in the Eocene,
sixty million years ago, that
may have been ancestral to
all the others. And then
there were all sorts of
lemurs, mostly living on Madagascar
where, protected from the
evolutionary competition of the
continents, they have developed a
whole array of special forms.
What does this tell us
about man? Not much, directly.
The more we know about
the anatomy and behavior
of these various primates, the
richer background we have for
looking at the human experience.
But clearly the living primates
do not represent a surviving

record of a sequence from
tarsier to monkey to ape
to man. In anatomy, the
apes are most like men.
In tool-using and in
group organization, it seems
to me that the distantly
related New World monkeys
are more human-like.
But men, apes, and monkeys
have all been evolving at
the same time, changing and
modifying the characteristics of their
remote common ancestors. Evolution
in man may have gone
on at a faster rate
than in apes, characteristics
may have persisted in one
kind of animal and not
in another, but this is
not easy to judge. The
method of comparing different kinds
of living organisms is not,
in itself, an adequate basis
for reconstructing a plausible
evolutionary story, however rich
it may be in suggestions
of plots for that story.

We were crowded 400 strong
into a movie theater at Florence,
S.C. The picture told
the story of the San Francisco
Earthquake. While watching on the screen
scenes of the city going up
in flames, I started wheezing. "Look
here, now," I scolded myself, "you're

not so allergic to smoke that
the sight of it on a
screen brings on your asthma."
Just then an usher, a
keen-eyed boy scarcely out of
his teens, marched down the aisle
and mounted the stage. As
the picture cut off he
spoke with composure and authority.
Ladies and Gentlemen: A new ruling
requires that we practice fire drills
in movie houses just as
is done in public schools. This
is the time for our drill.
"The children in our audience know
how it is done. When
I imitate the clanging of a
gong let all the school children
here fall into line and march
out the aisle just as
they would in school. Let
every parent present with a
small child follow the school
children. After them the adults
must file out two abreast.
Everybody cooperate and let's see
how orderly we can make
our first fire drill. I'll count
to three, then sound the gong.
"One. Two. Three. Clang! Clang! Clang!"
Like clockwork the aisles filled
with children who marched quietly
out to the street. Behind
them marched mothers with babes
in arms or led by
the hand, looking amused as
if playing a new game.
By then I was sputtering, choking.
And I saw smoke oozing from
under the stairs leading to
the balcony. My first impulse was
to rush for the open,
but the calm voice of the

boy on the stage halted me.
"Clang! Clang!" he was still
saying. "Adults now. Follow the
lead of the children. Two-
and-two fall into the
aisle and march out. March!
March! March!" The boyish voice
made a time-keeping singsong.
I caught a bit of
the youth's brave spirit and,
wheezes and all, I fell in
with my aisle partner. That
75-foot walk to the
entrance seemed a hundred miles long.
As the last couples came to
the door I heard the brave
young voice back on the
stage announcing. "Well done! It
took us only ten minutes
to clear the last one out."
Five minutes later an astounded but
thankful crowd stood on the
opposite sidewalk and watched the blazing
theater roof cave in. Not one
human being was hurt; not
a dozen out of the
400 had even been alarmed
for not that many had
seen or smelled the smoke.
One level-headed young man had
saved a situation that could
have so easily led to
panic. It came to light
afterward that Woodrow Cook's
method of evacuating the Florence,
S.C., theater was entirely spontaneous.

From "Life in These United States" by Elizabeth Holladay, in *The Reader's Digest* (December 1948).
Reprinted with permission from *The Reader's Digest*.

The Price of Not Reading

Every week I receive letters from
readers wanting to know where they
can buy a certain book I
have mentioned in the column.
When I mentioned my own book
coming out last spring, I was
flooded (well, sprinkled) with queries
about where it could be bought.
Books are to be found
in book stores, just as
fish is found in fish
shops and flowers in flower shops.
A book store is a
retail establishment with a sign
"Books" on the door or window.
A few years ago, I
read that there are more blacksmiths
in America than book shops,
and I believe it. Many
small towns do not have
a single book shop, and
even a few cities
of considerable size have books available
only in the local department store.
And even good book shops today
find it difficult to stay
in business solely from the sale
of books—most of them
make more out of greeting cards
and such frippery than they
do out of the books
themselves. The only booming segment
of the business is textbooks,
because more people are being
educated here than ever before.
But we are far from a
literate public. Although we have the
largest student body in the world,
and our educational budget alone is
bigger than the total national budgets
of most countries, we are

not a nation of readers.
Sometime ago, a Gallup Poll
taken in the U.S. and
Great Britain disclosed that the
English people read about five times
as many books as we
do—to which our characteristic
American reply would probably
be: "If they're so smart,
why ain't they rich?"   But
if we're so busy becoming rich
that we don't get smart,
we're in for a nasty jolt.
Reading habits throughout all Europe—
even behind the Iron Curtain,
where books are carefully censored—
are far more widespread and
ingrained than in our country.
Education, to us, is largely something
you finish when you get
a diploma.   Thereafter, books are
read only for amusement, if
at all.   And this attitude is
the chief mark of the failure
in our educational system—for
unless our schooling leaves us with
a lifelong appetite for learning,
it has done nothing but
given us a work certificate.
As long as there remain more
places in our country where
you can get a horse shod
than a book bought, we
will be a primitive people,
no matter how large our Gross
National Product, how tall our buildings,
how mighty our engines of war.
"Those who do not understand the
past," warned Santayana, "are condemned to
repeat it."   And how can we
understand what we push out of
mind the minute we leave school?

From the *S. F. Sunday Examiner & Chronicle.*   Reprinted by permission of Sydney J. Harris and Publishers-Hall Syndicate.

S&C Selection
Starting Time _____

SEA

The sea was bitter cold. From the vast empty plains of
Siberia howling winds roared down to lash the mountains
of Korea, where American soldiers lost on patrol froze into
stiff and awkward forms. Then with furious intensity the
arctic wind swept out to sea, freezing even the salt spray
that leaped into the air from crests of falling waves.

Through these turbulent seas, not far from the trenches
of Korea, plowed a considerable formation of American
warships. A battleship and two cruisers, accompanied by
fourteen destroyers to shield against Russian submarines, held
steady course as their icy decks rose and fell and shivered
in the gale. They were the ships of Task Force 77 and
they had been sent to destroy the communist-held bridges
at Toko-ri.

Toward the center of this powerful assembly rode two
fast carriers, the cause of the task force and its mighty arm.
Their massive decks pitched at crazy angles, which for the
present made take-offs or landings impossible. Their planes
stood useless, huddled together in the wind, lashed down
by steel cables.

It was strange, and in some perverse way resolutely
American, that these two carriers wallowing in the dusk bore
names which memorialized not stirring victories but humiliating defeats, as if by thus publishing her indifference to
catastrophe and her willingness to surmount it, the United
States were defying her enemies. To the east, and farther
out to sea, rode the *Hornet*, whose predecessor of that name
had absorbed a multitude of Japanese bombs and torpedoes,
going down off Guadalcanal, while the inboard carrier, the
Savo, would forever remind the navy of its most shameful
defeat in history, when four cruisers sank helpless at Savo
Island, caught sleeping by the audacious Japanese.

Now, as night approached the freezing task force, the
bull horn on the *Savo* rasped out, "Prepare to launch air-

craft!" And it was obvious from the way her deck was arranged that the carrier already had some planes in the skies over Korea, and every man who watched the heaving sea wondered how those planes could possibly get back aboard.

The bull horn, ignoring such problems, roared, "Prepare to launch helicopter!" and although the deck pitched in abandon, rotors began to turn, slowly at first and then with lumbering speed.

Now the great carrier struck a sea trough and slid away, her deck lurching, but relentlessly the bull horn cried, "Move jets into position for launching," and the catapult crew, fighting for footing on the sliding deck, sprang swiftly into action, inching two heavy Banshees onto the catapults, taking painful care not to allow the jets to get rolling, lest they plunge overboard with some sudden shifting of the deck.

"Start jet engines," roared the insistent bull horn.

The doctor, who had to be on deck in case of crash, looked at the heaving sea and yelled to the crane operator, "They may launch these jets, but they'll never get 'em back aboard."

The craneman looked down from his giant machine, which could lift a burning plane and toss it into the sea, and shouted, "Maybe they're planning to spend the night at some air force field in Korea. Along with the ones that are already up."

But at this instant all ships of the task force swung in tight circles and headed away from the open sea, straight for the nearby cliffs of Korea, and when the turn was completed, the deck of the *Savo* mysteriously stabilized. The effects of wind and sea neutralized each other, and planes returning from the bombardment of Korea now had a safe place to land.

But before they could do so the bull horn cried eerily into the dusk, "Launch helicopter!" and the crazy bird, its two rotors spinning so slowly the blades could be seen, stumbled into the air, and the horn cried, "Launch jets!"

Then, as the great carrier rode serenely amid the storms, the catapult officer whirled one finger above his head and a tremendous, almost unbearable roar arose and twin blasts of heat leaped from each Banshee, burning the icy air more than a hundred feet aft. Now the officer whirled two fingers and the roar increased and white heat scorched the deck of the carrier and the twin engines whipped to a meaningless speed of 13,000 revolutions a minute and the Banshee pilot, forcing his head back against a cushion, saluted and the catapult officer's right hand whipped down and the catapult fired.

Nine tons of jet aircraft were swept down the deck at a speed of more than 135 miles an hour. Within less than 150 feet the immense Banshee was airborne, and by the time it reached the forward edge of the carrier, it was headed toward its mission. Four times the catapults fired and four times heavy jets leaped into the darkening sky and headed for the coastline of Korea.

As soon as they had left, the bull horn wailed, "Respot planes. On the double. We must recover the Korea jets immediately."

When this announcement was made thirty old-fashioned propeller planes were already lashed down on the after part of the flight deck in precisely that area needed for landing the jets which now appeared overhead. The prop planes had been stowed there to permit catapult take-offs, and now they must be moved forward. So on the wooden deck, swept by icy winds, hundreds of young men in varicolored uniforms sped to the task of clearing the landing space. Men in green stowed the catapult gear so that no remnant of the powerful machine was visible. Other men in yellow leaped upon the deck and began to indicate the course each plane must follow on its way to forward stowage. Dozens of tough young men in blue leaned their shoulders against the planes, swung them laboriously into position and pushed them slowly into the biting wind. In blazing red uniforms other men checked guns or fueled empty craft while plane captains in brown sat in cockpits and worked the brakes to prevent accident. Darting about through the milling, pushing, shouting deck hands three-wheeled jeeps of vivid yellow and lumbering tractors in somber gray hurried to their jobs, while over all towered the mighty arms of the enormous black and sinister crane. Behind it lurked two weird men in fantastic suits of ashen gray asbestos, their faces peering from huge glassine boxes, ready to save the pilot if a crashed plane should burn, while in back of them, clothed in snowy white, the doctor waited, for death was always close upon the carrier deck.

So in an age of flight, in the jet age of incredible speed, these men pushed and pulled and slipped upon the icy deck and ordered the heavy planes with their bare hands. Upon trailing edges burdened with ice they pushed, their faces open to the freezing wind, their eyes heavy with frozen salt and the knuckles of their hands covered long since with protecting scars. And as they moved, their bright colors formed the pattern of a dance and after they had swarmed upon the deck for some minutes the *Savo* was transformed and from the lowering shadows the jets prepared to land.

This intricate operation was guided by one man. From the admiral's country he had directed the task force to run toward the communist coast. The last four jets had been dispatched at his command. He had placed the ships so that the operations of one would not trespass the allotted space of the other, and it was his responsibility to see that his carriers faced the wind in such position that smoke trailed off to one side rather than directly aft and into the faces of incoming pilots. Now he stood upon his bridge and watched the mountains of Korea moving perilously close.

Admiral George Tarrant was a tall narrow man with a sharp face that was sour and withdrawing like those of his Maine ancestors. Battle-wizened, he had fought the Japanese with his own carrier at Saipan, at Iwo Jima and at Okinawa, where his austere and lonely presence had brought almost as much terror to his own fliers as it had to the enemy.

He was known through the navy as George the Tyrant, and any aviator who wanted to fetch a big laugh would grab a saucer in his left hand, a coffee cup in his right, lean back in his chair and survey the audience sourly, snorting, "Rubbish." Then the mimic would stare piercingly at some one pilot, jab the coffee cup at him and growl, "You, son. What do you think?"

But men who served with Tarrant soon forgot his tyranny and remembered his fantastic skill in operating a task force. His men said flatly, "He can do it better than anyone else in the world." He knew the motion of the sea and could estimate whether a morning swell would rise to prevent recovery of afternoon planes or subside so that even jets could land freely. He was able to guess when new gales of bitter Siberian air would rush the line of snowstorms out to sea and when the snow would come creeping softly back and throw a blizzard about the task force as it slept at night.

And he had a most curious ability to foresee what might trouble the tin-can sailors serving in the remote destroyers.

He fought upon the surface of the sea and in the sky. He sent his planes inland to support ground troops or far out to sea to spot Russian submarines. His was the most complex combat command of which one man's mind was capable and on him alone depended decisions of the gravest moment.

For example, the position he was now in, with mountains closing down upon him, was his responsibility. Early that morning his aerologist had warned, "Wind's coming up, sir. You might run out of ocean by late afternoon."

He studied the charts and growled, "We'll make it."

Now his navigator warned, "We can't hold this course more than sixteen minutes, sir." The young officer looked at the looming coastline as if to add, "After that we'll have to turn back and abandon the planes."

"We'll make it," Tarrant grumbled as his ships plowed resolutely on toward the crucial hundred fathom curve which he dare not penetrate for fear of shoals, mines and submarines. But he turned his back upon this problem, for he could do nothing about it now. Instead, he checked to be sure the *Savo's* deck was ready and in doing so he saw something which reassured him. Far aft, standing upon a tiny platform that jutted out over the side of the carrier, stood a hulking giant, muffled in fur and holding two landing-signal paddles in his huge hands. It was Beer Barrel, and if any man could bring jets surely and swiftly home, it was Beer Barrel.

He was an enormous man, six feet three, more than 250 pounds, and his heavy suit, stitched with strips of flourescent cloth to make his arms and legs easier to read, added to his bulk. He was a farmer from Texas who before the perilous days of 1943 had never seen the ocean, but he possessed a fabulous ability to sense the motion of the sea and what position the carrier deck would take. He could judge the speed of jets as they whirled down upon him, but most of all he could imagine himself in the cockpit of every incoming plane and he seemed to know what tired and jittery pilots would do next and he saved their lives. He was a fearfully bad naval officer and in some ways a disgrace to his uniform, but everyone felt better when he came aboard a carrier, for he could do one thing. He could land planes.

He could reach out with his great hands and bring them safely home the way falconers used to bring back birds they loved. In the Pentagon they knew he broke rules and smuggled beer aboard each ship he served upon. Carrier captains knew it, and even Admiral Tarrant, who was a terror on navy rules, looked the other way when Beer Barrel staggered back after each drunken liberty, lugging his two ridiculous golf bags. The huge Texan had never once played golf and the two clubs sticking out were dummies. Once a deck hand, fearful that drunken Beer Barrel might slide back down the gangplank, had grabbed one of the outsize golf bags to help, but the surprising weight of it had crumpled him to the deck. Beer Barrel, barely able to heft the bag himself, had got it onto his massive shoulder, whispering beerily to the boy, "Thanks, Junior, but this is man's work." And he had carried the bags full of beer into his quarters.

For he believed that if he had a can of cold beer in his belly it formed a kind of gyroscope which made him unusually sensitive to the sea and that when this beer sloshed about it harmonized with the elements and he became one with the sea and the sky and the heaving deck and the heart of the incoming pilot.

"Land jets!" moaned the bull horn.

"Let's hear the checks," Beer Barrel said to his spotters, staring aft to catch the first jet as it made its 180° turn for the cross leg and the sharp final turn into the landing run. Now the jet appeared and Beer Barrel thought, "They're always pretty comin' home at night."

"All down!" the first watcher cried as he checked the wheels, the flaps and the stout hook which now dangled lower than the wheels.

"All down," Beer Barrel echoed unemotionally.

"Clear deck!" the second watcher shouted as he checked the nylon barriers and the thirteen heavy steel wires riding a few inches off the deck, waiting to engage the hook.

"Clear deck," Beer Barrel grunted phlegmatically.

He extended his paddles out sideways from his shoulders, standing like an imperturbable rock, and willed the plane onto the deck. "Come on, Junior," he growled. "Keep your nose up so's your hook'll catch. Good boy!" Satisfied that all was well, he snapped his right paddle dramatically across his heart and dropped his left arm as if it had been severed

clean away from his body. Instantly the jet pilot cut his
flaming speed and slammed his Banshee onto the deck. With
violent grasp the protruding hook engaged one of the slightly
elevated wires and dragged the massive plane to a shuddering
stop.

Beer Barrel, watching from his platform, called to the
clerk who kept records on each plane, "1593. Junior done
real good. Number three wire." Never did Beer Barrel
feel so content, not even when guzzling lager, as when one
of his boys caught number three wire. "Heaven," he explained once, "is where everybody gets number three wire.
Hell is where they fly wrong and catch number thirteen
and crash into the barrier and burn. And every one of you's
goin' straight to hell if you don't follow me better."

From his own bridge, Admiral Tarrant watched the jets
come home. In his life he had seen many fine and stirring
things: his wife at the altar, Japanese battleships going down,
ducks rising from Virginia marshes and his sons in uniform.
But nothing he knew surpassed the sight of Beer Barrel
bringing home the jets at dusk.

There always came that exquisite moment of human
judgment when one man—a man standing alone on the remot-
est corner of the ship, lashed by foul wind and storm—had
to decide that the jet roaring down upon him could make
it. This solitary man had to judge the speed and height
and the pitching of the deck and the wallowing of the sea
and the oddities of this particular pilot and those additional
imponderables that no man can explain. Then, at the last
screaming second he had to make his decision and flash it
to the pilot. He had only two choices. He could land the
plane and risk the life of the pilot and the plane and the
ship if he had judged wrong. Or he could wave-off and
delay his decision until next time around. But he could
defer his job to no one. It was his, and if he did judge
wrong, carnage on the carrier deck could be fearful. That
was why Admiral Tarrant never bothered about the bags
of beer.

On they came, the slim and beautiful jets. As they
roared upwind the admiral could see their stacks flaming.
When they made their far turn and roared downwind he
could see the pilots as human beings, tensed up and ready
for the landing that was never twice the same. Finally,
when these mighty jets hit the deck they weighed well over

seven tons and their speed exceeded 135 miles an hour, yet
within 120 feet they were completely stopped and this miracle was accomplished in several ways. First, Tarrant kept
his carriers headed into the wind, which on this day stormed
in at nearly 40 miles an hour, which cut the plane's relative
speed to about 95 miles. Then, too, the carrier was running
away from the plane at 11 miles an hour, which further
cut the plane's speed to 84, and it was this actual speed
that the wires had to arrest. They did so with brutal strength,
but should they miss, two slim nylon barriers waited to drag
the plane onto the deck and chop its impetus, halting it
so that it could not proceed forward to damage other planes.
And finally, should a runaway jet miss both the wires and
the barriers, it would plunge into a stout nylon barricade
which would entwine itself about the wings and wheels and
tear the jet apart as if it were a helpless insect.

But it was Beer Barrel's job to see that the barriers
and the barricade were not needed and he would shout curses
at his pilots and cry, "Don't fly the deck, Junior. Don't
fly the sea. Fly me." An air force colonel watching Beer
Barrel land jets exclaimed, "Why, it isn't a landing at all!
It's a controlled crash." And the big Texan replied in his
beery voice, "Difference is that when I crash 'em they're
safe in the arms of God."

C Test   Sea
Finishing Time _____
WPM _____

---

1   The two American carriers, *Savo* and *Hornet,* had names that memorialized

   a. stirring victories.

   b. great naval heroes.

   c. humiliating defeats.

   d. none of the above.

2   When the announcement was made that the jets were to be launched, the men wondered

   a. how the planes could possibly get back aboard.

   b. which of them would be selected to fly the mission.

   c. how great a distance they would have to fly.

   d. how important the mission was.

3 Tarrant, the admiral of the ship,

   a. was known as George the Tyrant.

   b. was an extremely able leader.

   c. looked the other way when Beer Barrel broke the rules about beer on board.

   d. is described by all of the above.

4 Beer Barrel

   a. was demoted when he didn't return to the ship on time.

   b. was an avid golfer.

   c. believed that beer improved his ability to land the jets.

   d. was disappointed when one of the pilots caught the number three wire.

5 The thirteen heavy steel wires on the deck were used to

   a. keep the jets in line at take-off.

   b. slow down and stop the jets at landing.

   c. mark the landing strips on deck.

   d. keep equipment from sliding off of the deck.

6 The speed of the jets at landing was cut down by

   a. heading the carrier into the wind.

   b. running the carrier away from the plane.

   c. engaging a hook from the jet into a steel wire on deck.

   d. all of the above.

7 Before the war, Beer Barrel had been

   a. a Texas farmer.

   b. a gambler.

   c. a cross-country truck driver.

   d. a bartender.

8 Beer Barrel believed that beer in his belly

   a. formed a kind of gyroscope which made him sensitive to the sea.

   b. made him harmonize with the elements.

c. made him one with the heart of the incoming pilot.
d. did all of the above.

CS = Total number correct _____ × *12.5 =* %

Sample Written Recall for the S&C Selection, "Sea"

Main idea: difficulties and dangers of landing jets on an aircraft carrier during Korean war.

Ship deck is heaving; slippery. Wind is strong; weather is cold; pilots are tired; fuel is low; Pilots must follow the signal man called Beer Barrel. Beer Barrel has to consider many factors for the landing. The admiral has to make complicated decisions. Beer Barrel believes that beer in his stomach makes him better able to land the planes. Decks have to be specially arranged for catapulting the jets off deck; then rearranged for landing them. Planes land by hooking into wires.

S&C Selection
Starting Time _____ .

WILD RICE

There are many legends and stories about how wild rice
came to the Indian people, but this is the one I like best.
In the days of long ago, it was the custom for the chief
to send young boys approaching manhood into the woods
to live alone and prove their strength and courage. They
existed on berries, roots, and anything they could find, and
were told to stay out many days. Sometimes they wandered
very far, got lost, and did not return. During these long
and lonely journeys, spirits spoke to them and they had
dreams and visions from which they often chose a name.
If they returned, they became hunters and warriors, and in
time took their places in the councils of the tribe.

One year a young boy wandered farther from the village
than all the rest. It was a bad time for berries and fruits
and he was sick from eating the wrong kinds. This boy
loved all that was beautiful and, though hungry, always
looked about him for flowers and lovely plants. One night
in a dream, he saw some tall, feathery grass growing in a
river. More beautiful than any he had ever seen, it changed
color in the wind like the waves on a lake. Upon awakening
he went to the river and there was the grass, tall and shining
in the sunlight. Though starved and weak, he was so impressed that he waded into the river, pulled some plants
from the mud, wrapped their roots in moss and bark, and
started at once toward the village.

After many days he saw the tepees before him and when
at last he showed what he had found, his people were happy
and planted the still wet roots in a little lake nearby where
it grew for several years until it became a field of waving
grass in the bay. One fall a wise old Indian, who had traveled
in many countries and knew all things, came to visit the
village. He was taken to the lake to see the beautiful tall
grass one of their young men had found. Seeing it, he was
amazed, raised his arms high and cried in a loud voice:

"Manomen—Manomen—a gift from the Manito."

He explained that the seeds were good to eat, showed them how to gather it and separate the chaff from the grain. Before he left, he advised them to plant it everywhere, guard it well, and use it forever. The Indians have never forgotten—and now all over the north country it grows in golden fields.

In the old days each family had a portion of a rice field as its own, outlined by stakes and established as a claim long before the rice was ripe. Sometimes as an aid in harvesting, and to protect the grain from the ever present threat of being blown off by the wind, the Indians tied it into small sheaves. Basswood fiber was used, one length fastened to another until a large ball was made. The ball was placed on a birchbark tray behind the woman doing the tying, one end of the fiber going over her shoulder through a birchbark loop to her hand. As the canoe was pushed through the rice, she gathered it in with a hoop and with a deft motion tied it together. The rows were long, their straightness a matter of pride. Now the rice was claimed, and safe from the storms.

At harvesting time, a camp was set up on the shore of a lake or river where wild rice grew; often several families banded together. Equipment was simple: canoes propelled by long, forked poles, rice-beating sticks, birchbark, woven matting of cedar, canvas, kettles or tubs from parching, trays for the winnowing, bags or bark containers for storage.

Few food supplies were taken along on these expeditions, the natives depending almost entirely on rice with fish, game, and berries; maple sugar from the spring gathering was often the only seasoning. At night the women set their nets and in the morning drew them out. If fishing were good, drying and smoking racks were set up and fires kept going constantly. The men hunted the fat, rice-fed ducks, shot moose, bear, or deer wherever they could find them. Snares were set for rabbits and partridge, blueberries were picked and dried, a great supply of food laid by for the all important days when harvesting took all their time.

Each day after work around camp was done, they started for the rice fields, usually not to return until midafternoon. A canoe full of rice was considered a day's harvest if there were any distance to go, but if the field were close, several loads could be picked in a day.

Warm, still days were ideal for harvesting, as winds and rain could ruin an entire crop within an hour, a catastrophe not unknown. This was the reason for tying the heads, for then the storms could come without danger of losing all. Not all the rice was picked; some was left for seed and some for the ducks, who were not only good to eat, but planted the rice, as they believed, in many places.

In small camps the parching and threshing was done in the afternoon and evening, and those who did the harvesting assisted; but in large camps where several families worked together, this all important activity was carried on by trusted experts who did nothing else.

Some years ago, in early September, I carried my canoe across the Basswood portage to Hula Lake where I knew the Indians were camped. Long before I reached the tents and tepees along the shore, I could smell the rich pungence of the parching fires, for their haze hung over the woods and blended with that of fall. Just before I reached the camp I stopped and rested my canoe in the crotch of a tree. A dog barked—someone was chopping—and then I heard what I was listening for, the modulated voices of Chippewas talking. It was a pleasant sound, rising and falling, an obligato to the rustling of leaves and to the lazy smoke drifting through the trees, part of the hush which seems to lie over the rice beds before they turn to gold.

Continuing the portage, I walked through the camp, dropped my canoe at the landing and returned. The men were sitting around resting and smoking after their day in the rice fields, women tended parching kettles, some tossed winnowing trays in an open place. Over a central fire was a tripod of white birch poles and from it hung a great iron kettle. An old woman was stirring and the fragrance of a wild rice stew made me hungry for the evening meal. Just beyond, another woman was chopping wood. Dogs and children ran happily about. Some canoes were still out, others returning loaded to the gunwales with green rice.

The field lay greenish gold in the light and the aspen where the camp was pitched took up the color, deepened and spread it all over the shore. Flocks of ducks were over the rice with a constant movement and flashing of wings; they paid little attention to the harvesters. Mostly black ducks, they were heavy and sluggish with the rice they had been gorging. When canoes came close, the ducks rose reluctantly to alight a short distance away, only to hurdle the canoes on their flight back. The harvest of succulent water-soaked kernels on the bottom was also theirs. Already fat as butter, they had a flavor no other fowl could equal.

David Thompson, a famous explorer in the late seventeen hundreds, spoke not only of the rice but of the ducks, stating in his diary:

"Mr. Sayer and his Men passed the whole winter on wild rice and maple sugar, which keeps them alive, but poor in flesh. It was a weak food, those who live for months on it enjoy good health, are moderately active, but very poor in flesh."

However, when he wrote about the ever present ducks, he was more enthusiastic for he said, they "become very fat and well tasted."

Had he known what the Indians knew, that wild rice must be eaten with fish, game, bear fat, or mixed with berries, to be a complete food, he might have changed his opinion of its nutrient value.

The scene before me had a certain timelessness. Except for the fact that Indians now had iron kettles, canvas, and modern tools, instead of birch-bark canoes, matting, and utensils made of cedar and other woods, it was little different from the age of copper and stone. These people were enjoying themselves. Rice gathering was never work, it was the occasion for a festival, with a sense of good feeling and industry that seemed to permeate the camp, the sea of tall grass out on the lake, and the very air itself.

I paddled out where some of the canoes were still harvesting. Joe and Frances were working down one of their rows, Joe poling the canoe, Frances using her rice sticks to gather in the grain. I sat quietly, watching. What a smooth and even rhythm, first the bending of the stalks to the gunwale, then a stroke with the beating stick, never a waste motion, the action almost hypnotic in its effect. Already there were several inches of the long, green kernels on the bottom. In a short time they would be ready to return.

"Good rice," said Joe without stopping the movement of his pole, "nice big rice and clean."

He leaned down, held up a handful for me to see, let it run between his fingers into the canoe, I paddled close, felt it myself. The kernels were long and heavy, as fine a crop as I had ever seen.

"I save some for you," he said, and that fall it was his bag of rice that hung from my rafter.

Later I followed the canoes back to camp and watched the preparations. First the green rice was spread on canvas in partial shade where the sun would not shine on it directly. Heating and mold could destroy it so it was stirred and dried evenly, a process that took most of a day depending on the weather.

After the first drying, the rice was parched, over a slow fire, in a large kettle or tub placed in a slanting position so it could be stirred by someone sitting beside it. The heat was carefully regulated, but skill was required so the kernels did not burn or scorch. The quantity done at one time was seldom more than a peck and it usually required an hour before it was finished. The woman doing this work felt her responsibility, for a moment's neglect or carelessness could destroy the work of many hours. She wielded her slender stirring paddle with a sense of importance, knowing the contents of her kettle might be the last should a storm or wind blow up before the harvest was finished.

Parching loosened the husks and imparted a smoky flavor to the rice. The paddle went round and round, through the rice and underneath, never still for a moment. A stick at a time was pushed into the fire, no large ones or any that might flame. The heat must be constant and slow.

But there was another and far more ancient process in use that day: green rice placed on a rack lined with marsh grass over a smoldering fire. Slower than the kettle method of parching, it dried the grain as one might dry vegetables, berries, or meat. This was "hard rice," greenish black when finished, requiring longer to cook. Keeping indefinitely, it was stored against emergencies and long trips.

After the rice was thoroughly parched by either process, it was put into a barrel or tub for the pounding which loosened the sharp husks and prepared the grain for treading. A wooden pestle, somewhat pointed at one end, was moved gently up and down near the edge of the mortar, never pushed, but allowed to drop of its own weight. It was considered an art to finish the pounding so most of the rice was whole. Broken and shattered grain was the mark of an amateur. While as good for eating as the other, something was lost in quality and appearance that was a matter of pride to the Chippewas.

The final step in the process was the treading to dislodge the fragments of husk. For this, a wooden receptacle holding about a bushel was partially sunk in the ground. A strong cross-pole was tied between two trees at a height of about four feet directly in front of it. The treading was done by a young man wearing a clean pair of new moccasins especially made for this purpose and tied tightly around the ankles. The sole of the foot, so Indians believe, is particularly adapted to this work, is soft, gentle, and firm in its movements.

I watched a man do this all important work; his treading like that of a dancer, his entire being in action. Leaning on the cross-pole and taking the weight off his feet, his body moved with undulating rhythm and sinuous grace. He felt the rice beneath his feet, massaged it, turned it over, almost caressed it in his attempt to separate the precious kernels from their hard and flinty husks. Before the days of wooden tubs, a hole was dug in the ground and lined with deer skin, but the process was exactly the same, a work of care, devotion, and artistry. Many Indians look with favor on the old ways, feel that to deviate too much from ancient customs means a loss not only in flavor, but in the meaning of the food.

After the treading came the winnowing and for this the threshed rice was carried to an open place where wind could sweep away chaff and hulls. It was either tossed and caught in a tray or poured from a height onto a canvas underneath. If the wind was dry and strong, and if parching, pounding, and treading had been well done, the chaff was all blown away, leaving the greenish, black kernels clean and ready for use.

The finished product was now poured carefully into bags, sewn tightly, and placed under cover. Some was for sale to whites, or for trade with other Indians, but most was saved for winter food. Once birch bark or woven matting was used for containers, but now the bags are of burlap or canvas. Their contents were always precious and guarded well.

One night there was a dance, the rice or harvest dance. Everyone dressed for the occasion and there was much excitement and laughter. Kettles were steaming with new rice, game, and berries. The bags were placed under cover where all could see and admire them, for the harvest was almost over. This was a night to be happy and to thank the Manito for his largesse and for a fine harvest season.

After dark when everyone was fed and the fire built up, the drums began their rhythmic beating and the dancers took their places. At times only men danced in a circle around the fire, sometimes only women, often both, the usual stepping and stomping to the steady beat of the drums. That night after the dancing had gone on for several hours, I saw a young man, possibly more gifted and imaginative than the rest, begin to imitate the actions of the harvest, the motion of poling a canoe through the water, the graceful swinging of the rice sticks, the circular motion of the paddle in the parching, the dance of the treader holding on to his balancing pole, the final winnowing with a tray. Others soon followed the inspired one until there was much confusion, each attempting to interpret some part of the many aspects of harvesting and preparation. Finally, tiring, they relapsed into the ancient broken half-step of all native dances, a ritual looked forward to by all the band.

I have not seen a harvest dance for a long time now, and it is possible younger Indians do not remember, or if they do would think it old-fashioned and beneath their dignity to indulge, but those who have seen and taken part, cannot forget the deep joy and meaning of such celebrations.

In the fall when the rice harvest is on, I think of canoes going through golden fields of it against the blue of the water, the flash of ducks above and the whisper of their wings, the redolent haze from parching fires over some encampment. I remember the drums and the dancers under a big September moon, the soft voices of the Chippewas, the feeling of these Indian harvesters of the lake country for this gift of their Manito, long ago.

C Test   Wild Rice
Finishing Time _____
WPM _____

1 The author's favorite legend about the discovery of wild rice is that it was found by a

  a. young Indian boy who had wandered from his village.

b. family of Indians who had traveled across the plains.

c. visitor who was a stranger to the Indians.

d. young Indian maiden.

2 As storms were imminent during harvest time, the Indians insured against total loss of the crop by

a. putting birchbark tents over portions of the fields.

b. harvesting some of the rice early.

c. tying the rice into small sheaves.

d. none of the above.

3 The rice is parched

a. in the sun.

b. over a slow fire.

c. in brick ovens.

d. in large, flat pans.

4 The Indians who harvest the wild rice are

a. Iroquois.

b. Chippewas.

c. Apaches.

d. Mohawks.

5 One of the final steps in preparing the wild rice is the dislodging of fragments of husk. This is accomplished by

a. treading on the kernels.

b. shaking the kernels in huge sacks.

c. forcing the kernels through net-like cloth.

d. grinding the kernels.

6 A game bird that is common to the territory during harvest season is

a. partridge.

b. pheasant.

c. wild goose.

d. wild duck.

CS = Total number correct _____ × *16.6 =*   %

THE BIG BRAIN

The second week in March is a grievous time for millions of Americans. The 15th of March is the deadline for the Federal income-tax returns. This is a bad time in any country, but no other country has an income-tax form so wordy, niggling, and elaborate. This is because the Bureau of Internal Revenue, true to the American prejudice, lets everybody make himself out to be a special case. By this system, no two men, even in the same sort of job, and earning exactly the same salary, will pay the same amount of tax. The harrowing complications set in when you face the page marked "deductions." There are certain fairly simple categories. You may deduct all medical expenses that amount to more than five per cent of your gross income, unless you're over 65, when you may be ill at the government expense to the extent of $1,250. You may deduct contributions to charities. You may deduct the cost of drugs you got on prescription, the taxes you paid to your state last year, interest on mortgages and property taxes, and alimony—which is a major industry in the United States. You may deduct in New York our third and most annoying form of taxation— the city sales tax, which you pay whenever you go into a store to buy anything except food and medicine, almost everything that costs more than one dollar. This alone takes quite a lot of figuring. How often did I go to the movies, or buy a dishcloth, or a hat, a pair of overshoes for the children, a pencil, a restaurant meal over a dollar?

The Bureau of Internal Revenue and its horde of mathematical drones has lately added insult to injury. They have in several big cities installed electronic calculators—they look like a couple of big trunks open for packing, but are in fact already jammed with hundreds of vacuum tubes. They are the babies of the giant electronic computer—the so-called electronic brain—they have up at Harvard and in a display center here in New York.

It appears that of the income-tax returns made out and
dutifully posted before midnight of the 15th of March approximately one in four is incorrect. Most of these mistakes
it seems are errors made in the simple good faith of bad
arithmetic. Some of them indicate a constitutional inability
to follow the economic maze of the instructions. Some
however amount to cunning attempts to doublecross the
income-tax collector. The staff of the Bureau of Internal
Revenue is always described as "huge." But it is never huge
enough. For every income-tax return has to be scrutinized
and checked and amended. And then down the years winds
the dreary routine of writing insults, interviewing the taxpayer, checking his personal files of checkbooks, leases, and
so on. I say down the years, because if by a happy mischance
you paid more than you ought to, it's likely to be a year
or two before the Bureau can humanly get around to sending
you the refund. I was challenged about three years ago
on my 1946 income tax—they had just got around to me.
When we were through, after a feud conducted with hysteria
on my part and phlegm on theirs, it came out that they
owed me a hundred and seven dollars. They said they'd
send me a check. This was a prospect that kept me on
edge for about ten months. Then I settled into boredom,
then a cynical resignation. Two weeks ago, the check arrived. However, it was not for a hundred and seven dollars.
It was for a hundred and twelve. The difference was the
amount of interest that had accumulated. Our Government
of course is a good government, a just and famous system,
but it has a Biblical distaste for usury. And that's why they
decided to employ these little electronic brains.

What they do now is this: a corps of girls, human enough,
take your tax return and with a few well-chosen taps on
a keyboard reduce its hieroglyphics to a pattern of perfora-
tions on a regular business machine card. The card looks
roughly like a pocket calendar that has been punched over
and over by a very neat and conscientious train-conductor.
The girls then feed these cards into the machine at the rate
of eight hundred a minute. The machine tubes warm up.
A switch is thrown. The tubes or valves flicker and there
is a scurry of little lights across the machine panel, about
as swift as a falling star. Your tax return is checked, errors
discovered and corrected, necessary refund or extra payment
noted, and the amended form comes out with the offending

mistakes circled in red and the correct total printed. It would take a well-adjusted taxpayer, with a flair for differential calculus, about three days to do this calculation. Just to turn the knife in the taxpayer's wound, the machine does it all in a seventieth of a second.

If this is what baby can do, what is the function of the parent monster who was reared at Harvard? I went up to Madison Avenue the other afternoon to find out, to take a look at Poppa, whose full legal name is the Selective Sequence Electronic Calculator. It does not look like Boris Karloff in a coat of mail. It does not even look like a power-house, or a big radio set. It looks like a big and beautiful room. Which is all the more menacing because, to begin with, you have nothing to fight. There is a room, about as big as a hotel lobby. There are marble floors. The walls are nothing but three banks of vacuum tubes enclosed in sliding glass panels and framed in stainless steel. In the middle of the floor is a big unit that looks like a streamlined organ console. It is in fact called the console and is also in stainless steel. Here sit two girls over hundreds of switches. They throw a dozen of them and look over to one of the walls. Across the wall there is a flurry of lights. And one of the girls says, "Yeah, I guess it's all right." There are two other units on the floor, in stainless steel and glass. One introduces—on those same little business cards with holes in—the problem that's to be solved by this inaudible and invisible brain. Another unit, much like the first, is a printer that prints up the results in exquisite electronic typing. You'll be relieved to hear, as I was, that there *is* a problem being worked on. The silence is appalling. It is broken from time to time by a momentary chatter or buzz, like a dentist drilling around a cavity. That's the big brain actually at work.

What sort of problem does the brain figure out? Well, this machine naturally isn't interested in anything that would ever disturb an accounting department. For such trifles there is a little offspring called a Calculating Punch, with a mere twelve hundred tubes, which will do in one second flat any big business problem entailing adding, subtracting, multiplying, and dividing, with a couple of five-digit numbers that require, say, seventy-nine separate multiplications or sixty-five divisions. Adding and subtracting of course are not so slow.

No, the monster is reserved for the kind of equations that have to be worked out in the physical sciences. It just did a little job of atomic physics for Princeton University. I might be able to explain this more lucidly to you if the girl who outlined the problem to me had not been a beautiful girl. When you come in off the street to be greeted by this vision, you might think you were meeting a charming floorwalker. But she turned out to be a college graduate who majored in mathematics and then took the course in electronic calculation at a college the business machine company runs for its demonstrators. (The great brain, by the way, cannot tell you her telephone number.) She said that Professor Niels Bohr, the Danish physicist, announced to the scientific world the impressive theory—I'm told it's impressive—that the nucleus of a uranium atom was much like a drop of water and splits unevenly. The only snag in the way of this discovery was the prospect, or the probable certainty, that a drop of water splits evenly. You will simply have to take it on trust that to find out how drops of water behave would engage expert physicists in a calculation taking three generations to compute, or one very healthy mathematician about a hundred years. No point in following that line of thought then. But the Princeton physics department put it up to Poppa. One of the absurd and laughable things about Poppa is that although he can do inhuman subtraction and division—he can even carry four hundred thousand digits in his head stored up on hand in what's called a memory unit—you have to tell him exactly *when* to go into action on each step. He tends to sit around in the lobby like a house detective till the girl at the desk hands him a number. That's what takes the time—punching out those cards to tell him at what stage to add, when to switch to long division, when to square something, when to subtract. Poppa's quite a moron in his own fabulous way. However, they lined up the order of the sequence of problems and fed them into the banks of twinkling lights. And it took Poppa just less than four days—one hundred and three hours. Dr. Bohr, and the Princeton physicists, and the world of physics, knew the answer—surprise, surprise—a drop of water splits unevenly. They can now proceed with Dr. Bohr's earthshaking theory.

Poppa has also recently obliged the navy by computing the rate of shock wave reactions. He has done a very complicated problem set by an oil company: to figure out the effective rate of pumping to keep the oil pure of salt and mineral saturation. For an observatory he plotted in a day or two something that would have taken years and years—the orbits of five planets between 1780 and 1960. When I was there they had just finished printing up a vast calendar recording the location of the moon at midnight and midday for every day of the past hundred years. Some star-gazer was eager to know this—don't ask me why. Poppa was presently engaged on a problem slipped to him by the Atomic Energy Commission—a problem that no humans anywhere could even attempt. It was to take the brain five and a half months. Working, by the way, twenty-four hours a day, because if you switch off his power, the brain simply loses track of the four hundred thousand digits he's carrying in his memory unit (for use at various stages of a problem) and falls into a carefree coma indistinguishable from Dr. Einstein on a fishing trip. It takes days to warm him up again and get some sense back into him. (Incidentally, if ever the girls feel skittish or mad at him, they can throw the wrong switches, or overload a few tubes, and plug him into an actual nervous breakdown.)

Although Poppa is in great demand for government problems, he and his brood can be rented by private firms. In the spirit of our times, they are available to the government free of charge (for a dollar a year, that is) for the solution of military problems. But if you are a peace society who'd like to discover, say, a reliable formula for a quiet life, that—as Chico Marx once said—begins to run into money. I'm afraid in that case you'd have to hire Poppa at the regular rate of three hundred dollars an hour.

C Test   The Big Brain
Finishing Time _____
WPM _____

---

1   The phrase, "The Big Brain" refers to

  a. a large team of mathematicians in the Internal Revenue Service.
  b. an electronic computer.
  c. the consultants who service electronic computers.
  d. the physicists who use electronic computers.

2 The United States Government

    a. is prompt in refunding overpayments on income tax.

    b. employs a large staff of accountants to check income tax returns.

    c. uses electronic computers to check income tax returns.

    d. checks about one in every fifty income tax returns.

3 The Big Brain looks like

    a. the control tower at a large airport.

    b. a large room with a streamlined organ console in the middle.

    c. a large ultramodern building.

    d. a factory.

4 Dr. Niels Bohr used the computer to test the theory that the uranium atom

    a. is like a drop of water and splits unevenly.

    b. is perfectly symmetrical.

    c. has an elliptical structure.

    d. has positive and negative poles.

5 If the Big Brain is turned off, it

    a. takes days to warm it up again.

    b. loses track of the digits it is carrying in the memory unit.

    c. is indistinguishable from Dr. Einstein on a fishing trip.

    d. is described by all of the above.

6 The Big Brain is

    a. vital for the defense of the United States.

    b. used for simple but lengthy accounting tasks.

    c. reserved for the kind of equations that have to be worked out in the physical sciences.

    d. used only by private industry.

7 When the Big Brain is at work, it sounds like

    a. silence punctuated momentarily by a chatter or buzz.

    b. pneumatic drills.

    c. a steady and loud tapping.

    d. a steady and barely audible hum.

8 Of the income-tax return mailed before midnight of the fifteenth of March, approximately

   a. one in seven is incorrect.
   b. one in seven has an error that exceeds 2 percent underpayment or overpayment.
   c. one in four is incorrect.
   d. one in four has an error that exceeds 2 percent underpayment or overpayment.

9 According to the author, the most harrowing complications in making out income-tax returns occur when you

   a. calculate the exact amount of tax that you owe.
   b. face the page marked "deductions."
   c. decide that you are a special case.
   d. calculate interest rates on mortgage loans.

10 The Big Brain

   a. is available only for the solution of military problems.
   b. cannot be rented by firms other than government agencies.
   c. is available for one hundred thousand dollars a year to the government.
   d. is available for one dollar a year to the government.

CS = Total number correct _____ × *10 =*   %

S&C Selection

Starting Time _____

THE URGENCY OF LUNCH

The Washington social day begins with a conference and builds with relentless speed to the first climax, lunch. A Washington conference is much like a conference in any other city. Each man comes armed with an assortment of proposals cunningly contrived to make his colleagues sweat, and everyone kills a few hours dodging the hovering menace of responsibility. At the end, a committee is appointed.

When this ordeal ends, the conferee is free to start plotting his lunch. Only the callow will move frivolously at this stage, for here, as every Washington survivor instinctively knows, is the first crisis of the day, a test that can make or destroy the striver for status.

Remember, the important thing is seeming to be in the know. Unless you are one of the fortunates so powerful that you have boons to grant, being in the know is useless. People must *think* you are in the know!

How will they arrive at this conclusion? Certainly not by your telling them. If, for example, you are in elegant company and calmly state on your own authority that the President last week wrote a speech attacking Senator Survine but then burned it, you will arouse no one's interest. Your statement will probably be dismissed immediately as the fiction of a scheming brain. You may note in your listeners that impassive blinking of eyelids which means that they have recognized a lightweight.

But try dropping the same morsel in the following style: "I had lunch the other day with Jack McSweeney, who's helping to ghost the President's speeches. By the way, did you know that the President wrote a speech attacking Senator Survine and then burned it?"

This may not stop the party the first time it is tried, but it is certain to double your audience within the next eight seconds and provoke a few attempts to top you. These can easily be blasted now that the authenticity of your source

From *An American In Washington* by Russell Baker. Copyright © 1961 by Russell Baker. Reprinted by permission of Alfred A. Knopf, Inc.

is established. A supplementary clincher might go as follows: "I understand that the President was so furious about the mohair-subsidy bill that he took nine strokes on the fourth hole the other day."

Within forty-eight hours both of these items about the President will appear in famous metropolitan newspapers, solemnly garnished with explanations of their significance for next year's legislative program ("Prexy Reaches Breaking Point with Survive"; "Mohair Repealer Seen Certain"). Note that you have not actually said that Assistant Ghost McSweeney told you anything; you have merely stated that you had lunch with him the other day. In fact, you may have fabricated both items on the spur of a highball. No matter. From the audience viewpoint you have established yourself as a man in the know by the prefacing statement that you have lunched with McSweeney.

To pull this sort of coup regularly, it is obviously necessary to be seen lunching with McSweeney. It is foolhardy to be seen munching sandwiches at the People's drug counter or carrying a tray at Linda's Cafeteria. The ambitious will keep his lunch schedule filled with names suitable for dropping in the circle he wishes to conquer.

A good selection of lunch companions would include one member of the White House staff, a few Assistant Secretaries of State, a flag officer or two from the Pentagon, a scattering of senators, a famous pundit, a lawyer from the oil lobby, an economics professor on loan to the Treasury, three or four good ambassadors, and a mysterious friend from the Central Intelligence Agency. The last may be pure invention—possibly an old friend who rarely gets into town. The others can be lured to lunch on the pretext of extraordinary business to be discussed or on the strength of a casual introduction at any cocktail reception you may have crashed.

The chances are excellent that none will ever drop any indiscreet information, but this is irrelevant. Their presence across the lunch table will suffice to arm you with the authority needed to rise in Washington. Indeed, on the strength of the reputation that can be built, you may soon find these people calling *you* for lunch in the hope of profiting from being seen in your company. On days no one can be brought to table it is helpful, if one's employer or competitive colleagues are in earshot, to telephone the office of an unusually gaudy personage and tell his secretary that you would like to speak to her boss sometime at his convenience about lunching with you. She will promise to set up a telephone conversation for you—one of these days.

The importance of lunch grows from the universal hunger for communication within a city where it is rapidly becoming impossible to understand anything that is said for public consumption. Lunch is not so much a meal as a forum where men from different agencies and businesses can meet, trade tiny fragments of information, and try to puzzle out, from their clandestinely bartered clues, what is going on.

Its intimacy breeds confidence and makes it immensely more important as a social function than the overpublicized cocktail circuit. Its protocol demands at least a token exchange of confidences about what is really happening inside the bureaucratic warrens along the river front. In a city where most official utterances are deliberately phrased to mislead, evade, or seduce, it is a reliable communication medium where a few men can at least try to explain honestly what the score is.

And so, thousands and thousands of telephone calls crisscross the city each morning in a groping for human contact away from the roar of the mimeograph machines and the hollow thunder of ghost-written inanities. Interestingly, the one place in town where lunch is nothing more than it is in any other city—a perfunctory gesture to the stomach—is the Capitol. There are various plausible explanations. The most persuasive is the unspeakable cuisine of the House and Senate dining rooms.

C Test   The Urgency of Lunch

Finishing Time   _____

WPM   _____

---

1   A Washington conference is similar to conferences in other American cities in that

   a. new ideas are proposed and evaluated.

   b. a committee is appointed.

   c. decisions are reached through democratic means.

   d. one man always tries to dominate.

2 The important thing for one who strives for status in Washington is to be

    a. a large contributor to campaigns.

    b. in a position to make frequent speeches.

    c. in the know.

    d. able to make people think you are in the know.

3 The way to persuade people that your "inside information" is true is best accomplished by

    a. prefacing your statement with the fact that you had lunch with your well-placed source of information.

    b. making statements that are so far-fetched that everyone thinks they must be true.

    c. making your statements in a very casual way.

    d. establishing a reputation as a good political analyst.

4 To pull the "lunch" routine regularly, you must frequently be seen having lunch

    a. at expensive restaurants.

    b. in the senators' dining room.

    c. with old friends.

    d. with a variety of important people.

5 The reason that lunch is so important in Washington is that it

    a. is the one place where reliable political communications can be made.

    b. permits lobbyists to make numerous contacts.

    c. gives congressmen a chance to consult with their visiting constituents.

    d. provides the only break during a politician's long and busy day.

CS = Total number correct _____ × *20 =*   %

Speed Test

Starting Time _____

A SHORT HISTORY OF SURFING

Swimming as a sport was almost unknown in the early history of mankind, and it was not until the days of the Egyptians, 4000 years ago, that we have records of man being able to swim.

Swimming was highly rated in the days of ancient Greece and Rome and practised in the training of warriors for fighting. However it was generally discontinued in Europe in the Middle Ages, as it was thought that outdoor bathing helped to spread the terrible epidemics of various diseases which swept the Continent. It was not until half-way through the nineteenth century that swimming started again as a sport and recreation in Europe.

The sailors manning the ships of Cook, and the first navigators of the South Seas have left records of the daring of the natives as swimmers and surfers. Almost two hundred years ago Cook wrote:

> On our way we came to one of the few places where access to the island is not guarded by a reef, and consequently a high surf breaks upon the shore; a more dreadful one I have seldom seen; it was impossible for any European boat to have lived in it, and if the best swimmer in Europe had been by accident exposed to its fury, I am confident that he would not have been able to preserve himself from drowning; yet in the midst of these breakers were ten or twelve Indians swimming for their amusement. Whenever a surf broke over them they dived under it, and to all appearances with infinite facility rose again on the other side.

In another part of his Journal of the first voyage the great seaman describes the skill with which the Tahitians shot the waves to the shore, using a piece of an old canoe which they found in the vicinity. Such practices must have filled both captain and crew with surprise and awe, as most sailors could not swim and made no attempt to learn. They knew that if they fell overboard while at sea they were dead men in any case, as the ungainly vessels of those days took a long time to wear round and approach the particular spot where a man might be struggling in the water. Often there was no attempt to turn the ship in such circumstances, so knowing how to swim would only postpone the victim's inevitable fate.

For many years after the coming of the white man to Australia, the beaches near Sydney were used only as tracks to the north and south of the settlement. Gradually, however, men began to explore the joys of sea bathing, until the prudery of the Victorian age produced edicts designed to stop such an indulgence. Accordingly it was pronounced that no person was to bathe "in waters exposed to view from any wharf, street, public place or dwelling house between the hours of 6 a.m. and 8 p.m."

Because of this edict hardy souls who persisted in bathing in the sea had to rise with the birds and pursue their pleasure in the early hours of the morning. A few of their womenfolk accompanied them, and were to be seen dipping in the waves on the edge of the sands, clad in home-made neck-to-knee costumes, usually of a material known as galatea, with embroidered edges, sleeves of elbow length, and the knee portions reinforced with elastic. The fair bathers usually had their legs covered in black cashmere stockings, with bathing shoes below, and a round beret-type hat on their heads.

Mixed bathing had always been prohibited in closed waters, but dividing up an open beach into sections according to sex was an impossibility.

Apparently Clovelly, one of Sydney's southern beaches, originally known as "Little Coogee," was the first place where mixed bathing was officially countenanced. Bathing-sheds were provided for changing, and this led to the consideration of similar demands at other beaches. Manly extended the time of bathing to 8 a.m. and installed a rough enclosure with a lattice top, for men to change in. Old hands remember the familiar costume of the day—neck-to-knee blue swimmers with a triangle fore and aft, worn over the costume, and known as "vees." These were trimmed with coloured braid, Manly being blue, North Steyne gold, Bondi white, and so on. Some of the younger bathers, with the idea of being different, bought "Canadian" costumes—

two-piece woollen affairs with coloured edges. Often an unexpected wave would cause the top half to part company with the lower, exposing a big expanse of flesh, front and back, and embarrassing the wearer.

Familiarity with the beaches came to breed a certain contempt of their dangers, and the better swimmers among the men began to try their strength and skill against the sea—a practice that led to disaster in a number of cases.

A visiting South Sea Islander, Tommy Tanna, is credited with introducing Sydney swimmers to the art of body-shooting on breakers. Tanna, who was employed as a gardener's boy at Manly, near Sydney, amazed onlookers by the way in which he could throw himself in the path of a wave and go hurtling towards the beach in the froth of broken water. Local surfers were quick to acquire this ability, and soon it was being practised on other beaches as well.

Gradually the ordinance forbidding bathing between prescribed hours became difficult to police, and its end came with a memorable act of defiance. On 1st September 1902 the editor of a Manly newspaper, W. H. Gocher, announced that he intended to bathe publicly outside the permitted hours. Seeking a test case, he advertised the intention in his newspaper. The following Sunday, at noon, he bathed on Manly's ocean beach, but no official action was taken, and as Gocher continued to bathe unmolested again and again on Sundays, the public quickly realized that the freedom of the beaches was ensured. Others in municipalities north and south of Manly followed Gocher's example, and the custom of surfing at any hour of the day was soon firmly established.

Finishing Time _____
WPM _____

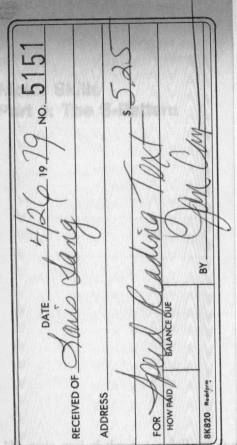

7

...s that you have practiced so far ... to set the stage for learning the S-pattern. This pattern resembles a series of Ss set end-to-end down the page. The Ss are formed within the confines of the scan-reduction lines. Figure 5 illustrates the S-pattern.

The Spanish government wasn't too happy to have the United States on the frontier of Texas. The frontier itself was a possible cause of trouble. It was not clear exactly what Napoleon had sold to Jefferson and whether or not the purchase included Texas. A good many Americans were of the opinion that they had bought Texas from Napoleon. To prevent clashes between Americans and Spaniards a kind of no man's land had been established, but this became a haven for outlaws and land grabbers who waited for any excuse to cross the border.

Figure 5. The S-Pattern

SOURCE: From *Remember the Alamo!*, by Robert Penn Warren. Copyright © 1958 by Random House, Inc. Reprinted by permission of the publisher.

Eye movements for the S-pattern must be developed gradually. The hand is to move as if following imaginary Ss drawn down the page, and the eyes are to follow the hand. Initial practice with the S-pattern should begin with columns of six to eight words in width, somewhat narrower than the ordinary printed page. Readings for beginning practice with the S-pattern are included in this chapter.

When you first use the S-pattern, use your entire hand to guide your eyes. Your fingers should be approximately perpendicular to the line of print. Place your hand on the left side of the page, under the first line. Move your hand to the right and down at the same time and follow this movement with your eyes. Move down across three lines by the time you reach the word at which the right-hand scan-reduction line would be drawn (see Figure 5). Similarly, as you move from the right side of the page back to the left, move gradually down the page for a total of three lines. In effect, your hand and eyes make a diagonal movement across three lines. This is referred to as a three-line S-pattern and is the one illustrated in Figure 5. The S-pattern may be modified so that your eyes will traverse greater vertical distances with each horizontal movement across the page; that is, movement down the page can be increased from three, to four, to five lines, and so on. At the outset, practice the three-line S-pattern until your hand and eyes become quite adept at the movement and you are able to comprehend the material easily as you read. Then gradually increase the number of vertical lines crossed in a single left-to-right movement. In addition, work toward decreasing the amount of left-to-right eye movement. You can train yourself to rely more and more on peripheral vision by imagining the two scan-reduction lines closer and closer to the center of the page. A series of exercises has been developed to facilitate mastery of the S-pattern. Instructions for these exercises follow.

Read the first selection that follows ("Why the Spaniards Were Afraid") at a very rapid rate using the line-by-line, hand-eye technique. The purpose of this reading is to familiarize yourself with the content of the passage. After the first reading, go back to the beginning of the passage and use the S-pattern to reread the entire selection. Your primary goal on the first readings with the S-pattern is to learn to follow your hand as it traces the pattern. Try to understand the material as you read, but do not worry about your level of understanding. Write your recall of the passage. Reread the passage four times using the S-pattern and gradually increase your speed with each new reading. Add to your written recall after each reading.

Continue practice with the S-pattern on the other selections provided. Begin with a line-by-line reading, and move smoothly through the passage to gain some familiarity with it. Do not time yourself, and move at a comfortable rate. Then go through the passage three or more times using the S-pattern. You will find that the pattern becomes easier to use each time and that you can increase your speed with very little effort. The purpose at this point is to achieve speed and smooth motion with the S-pattern. Familiarity with the material through numerous readings reduces the chance that you will slow down.

When you practice the S-pattern in reading your practice book, read each passage at least three times, employing written recall after each reading. Experience has shown that students are able to transfer the S-pattern to new material more easily when they have used the pattern over and over again on well-understood passages. Do not underestimate the usefulness of this procedure. Be sure to use repeated readings of the same passages to build up speed with the S-pattern.

When you first apply the S-pattern to S&C selections, you may observe a decrease in reading speed. This is not unusual. Each time you learn a new technique, the time it takes to concentrate on the new movement adds to the reading time. After several hours of practice with the S-pattern, however, you will find that your reading speed on new material surpasses your previous level. By recording your scores on each S&C selection and on outside readings, you will have an accurate gauge of the amount of progress you have made. A temporary decline in speed or comprehension is no cause for alarm.

Why the Spaniards Were Afraid

The Spanish government wasn't too happy
to have the United States on
the frontier of Texas. The frontier
itself was a possible cause of
trouble. It was not clear exactly
what Napoleon had sold to Jefferson
and whether or not the purchase
included Texas. A good many Americans
were of the opinion that they
had bought Texas from Napoleon. To
prevent clashes between Americans and Spaniards
a kind of no man's land
had been established, but this became
a haven for outlaws and land
grabbers who waited for any excuse
to cross the border.
There was another cause of trouble
besides the disagreement about the border
line. The Spanish could not help

but contrast their own failure to
settle Texas with the splendid success
of the American expansion westward. The
Spaniards knew what the American frontiersman
was like, and how he moved
into new land like water running
downhill. In one way, their worry
was not so much about the
policy of the United States government
toward Texas and the line. It
was the worry that the United States,
even if it wanted to
respect the Texas border, would not
be able to restrain the movement
of the frontiersmen toward new, unoccupied
land.
It has been said that those frontiersmen
had no cowards or weaklings among
them, for the cowards had never
started and the weaklings never got
there. This is not true, of
course. But they were men brought
up to hardship and danger, with
pride in their manhood, and there
were enough of them who were
not cowards or weaklings to give
the Spanish government some cause for
worry.
It was not just the frontiersman's
toughness that the Spanish worried about.
The Spanish themselves were tough. They
had faced terrific hardship and had
conquered a continent. But the American
frontiersman had something besides his toughness.
He was an individualist. He might
pick up his long rifle, whistle
to the bear dogs, and head
off into the wilderness, followed by
his wife and children, who rode
on a couple of ponies with
a few pots and pans. He
was "tarnation fool and consarn idiot
enough just to traipse out a

little farther, and durn them Indians."
Of course, he might get scalped.
But if he did get scalped,
there might well be a couple
of dead Indians somewhere with the
little lead pellet of the long
rifle deep in heart or brain.
And the next week, or the
next year, there would probably be
another settler there just like him,
and soon there would be another
cabin and corn patch among the
stumps of trees that had been
burned to make a place for
scratch farming. There would be a
hominy mill made out of a
scooped-out stump, and a heavy
wood chunk for bruising the grain
would hang on a thong from
a sapling. A bearskin would be
stretched on one wall of the
cabin. A path, already worn bare,
would lead down to a clear
spring. There would be, just inside
the door, a new cradle hollowed
out of a length of tulip
log, and a fiddle hung over
the fireplace where the evening pot
bubbled.
. . .
The Spanish feared the independence of
this kind of man, who would
get up and go somewhere without
waiting for anybody's say-so. And
they feared the kind of democracy
which these men practiced. The frontiersmen
couldn't get it out of their
heads that people ought to elect
their own government and that government
existed for the good of the
people. Many frontiersmen and other Americans
went to Texas with the honest
intention of becoming good Mexican citizens.

But they were ripe for trouble
when the Mexican government began to
change from what they thought a
government ought to be.
The notion of democratic government which
the honest American settler brought to
Texas wasn't the only thing to
make the pot of trouble boil.
Besides the honest settlers, there were
other Americans with an eye on
Texas.   These were the adventurers.
The small fry among these adventurers
might be nothing but border toughs—
part-time highwaymen of the sort
who infested the trails and traces
of the Mississippi Valley or former
river pirates who had decided
to try dry land.   Then, too,
there were the smugglers.   Spain did
not allow trade over the Texas
border, and so the illegal business
was very appealing to professional smugglers
and even to legitimate merchants who
had a little money to invest.
Nor was that all.   The plains
of Texas were full of wild
horses, any man's for the taking—
if he managed to keep his
scalp.   So there were the mustang
raids.
The big fry, however, were not
out to smuggle merchandise or run
mustangs over the border.   They had
big ideas.   They were out to
build nations, or steal empires.   They
were men like Aaron Burr, who
was arrested and tried for attempting
to seize the Mississippi Valley for
an empire of his own.   Or
General Wilkinson, who had the notion
of grabbing Louisiana and Texas.   Or
the famous highwayman Murrell, who built
up a far-flung secret organization

and dreamed of an empire of
outlaws. Or the even more famous
pirate Jean Lafitte.
But by the time of the
Louisiana Purchase there was more for
the Spanish government to worry about
than American adventurers. The people who
lived in Mexico—some of pure
Spanish blood, some of mixed Indian
and Spanish, and some of pure
Indian blood—had become restless under
Spanish rule. Rebellions began. It was
to be years before Mexico gained
her independence from Spain, but meanwhile
the fighting in Mexico gave new
excuse for Americans to come in.
Some of the Americans came with
the notion that they were helping
the cause of liberty by fighting
in a war like their own
Revolution. Some came because the war
gave opportunity for daring and cunning
men to become rich and powerful.
And some came with a mixture
of reasons.

Additional Practice with the S-Pattern

Science and Man

Which is more important for human
development, heredity or environment? This question
about "nature versus nurture" is the one
most often asked of the human geneticist.
It is far too crudely stated
to be of much value in
unifying the scientific understanding of man,
but we must find some
way of dealing with it—if
only because it is so often asked.
Before we can attempt to appraise the
scientific evidence, we have to clarify the
question. Then we can consider ways to
answer it. Both steps involve treacherous confusion.
By taking extreme examples, it is easy
to prove either side of the issue.
Men are almost always more resourceful than
monkeys. The essential difference between man
and monkey is heredity—the chemistry
of DNA molecules. Monkeys reared in the
most stimulating environment never approach human intelligence.
But it must be pointed out that
much of the difference—the culture
that includes language, agriculture, social organization,
industrial skills—comes from the environment
that man has created. It is
possible that only a small enlargement
of the monkey's brain, to facilitate
its speech, is all that stands
between it and the emergence of
new cultures analogous to the human.
In other circumstances, environment may be the
overriding factor. A fetus of impeccable genetic
quality may be so impaired by a
prenatal attack by German measles virus that
it cannot survive, or it does and
continues its distorted development, it may
have lost too many brain cells.
Man versus monkey, or brain-damaged versus

healthy, are extreme examples of hereditary and
environmental differentials, but the same principles apply
to the infinite gradation of subtler
differences in human heredity and experience.
The nature-nurture issue has no universal
answer; it must be looked at existentially.
If we see differences in performance
within a group of people, or
between groups, we can ask a
specific question about that group. Of
the total observed variability in IQ, income
or education in a group, what fraction
can we attribute to variations in heredity
and what fraction to variations
in environment?
If we also take into account the
interactions between the two terms, the
fractions must total 100 percent. Thus,
we could standardize the environment of
a given group and then all of
its variability would have to be genetic.
If we standardized the genetics—for example,
by dealing with identical twins—the
observed variability would have to be environmental.
If environment and heredity are both
variable as is almost always the case
in human affairs, we also have to
consider whether the two are optimally matched.
The nature-nurture issue has been
raised in the most pointed fashion in
connection with race. The performance of
Negroes in academic and economic competition in
the United States is an urgent
social problem. Sensibleness tells us we must
concentrate on individual performance, not group labels.
Nevertheless, it has been asserted that we
ought to narrow our expectation for
the ultimate catchup of minority races
because they might have some hereditary limitation.
We are not very knowledgeable about how
to identify the most crucial factors in
nurturing the intellectual and social development
of a child. However, one would

have to be studiously blind not to
see an ample explanation of racial
lag in the existing discriminatory environment.
But, the retort goes, it is well
known that a large part of
the differences in intelligence are hereditary; therefore
the minority groups must, to the same
extent, be genetically inferior. This is the
fraud of translating measurements in one homogeneous
group to predictions about inter-racial differences.
Until the environments are made comparable, or
until the whole process of the development
of intellect is scientifically well-understood, we
have no way to draw any conclusions
whatever about the nature of racial difference.
Fortunately, we are committed by law,
and by our confrontation with conscience and
reality, to make the experiment; to find
out how far human performance can be
liberated by removing the burden of discrimination.

From the *Washington Post*. Reprinted by permission of Joshua Lederberg and the *Washington Post*. Appeared in S. F. Chronicle Sunday Punch, August 25, 1968.

S&C Selection
Starting Time _____

THE ENGLISH LONGBOW

A classic example of the power of the English longbow, which has previously been mentioned, was the Battle of Crécy in northern France, August 26, 1346, during the Hundred Years' War. This battle, in which the longbow made its first appearance on the European continent, illustrates the effect the weapon had on medieval tactics.

Edward III of England, at the head of a raiding column, had crossed the Channel and attacked Normandy towns, looting and burning as he went. Informed that Philip VI of France was approaching with a hastily assembled army much larger than his own, Edward retreated toward the coast, hotly pursued by the French. The English were delayed by several river crossings; and as they approached the village of Crécy along a narrow forest track, Philip's forces gained on them rapidly.

When the English emerged from the woods, Edward decided to make a stand at the top of a sloping meadow beyond the trees. He divided his army into three "battles," as divisions were then called: one under his son Edward, the "Black Prince"; the second under two of his dukes; and the third, held in reserve in the rear, under his own command.

These first two battles drew up in line at the top of a small hill, overlooking the thick forest they had just traversed. The knights dismounted and formed in close order in the center of the line of each battle, while their horses were led to the baggage lines in the rear. Flanking the dismounted knights were two battalions of English longbowmen, their lines extending outward from the center like wings.

Groups of peasants were put to work preparing traps for the French cavalry. In front of the lines they scattered spiked obstructions called calthrops and dug trenches that were then camouflaged with brush and grass to make pitfalls.

Then the English sat down to wait. Presently there was movement along the narrow forest track, and soon enemy crossbowmen emerged from the shadows and began deploying across the meadow. Just at this moment the sky darkened and a sudden violent thunder burst over both armies, drenching everyone. It lasted only a few minutes, and the sun soon reappeared.

The French van, made up of a large body of Genoese crossbowmen, advanced upon the English lines and fired a volley of bolts which fell short, possibly because their bowstrings had been wet by the rain. Then the English longbowmen, who had managed to keep their strings dry inside their tunics, opened fire. Clouds of deadly cloth-yardshafts whistled through the air in almost unbelievable numbers, and their greater range found the helpless Genoese with deadly accuracy. The crossbowmen faltered and broke, unable to withstand the hail of arrows, just as the first French knights appeared from the forest. Furious at what they believed to be rank cowardice on the part of their Genoese allies, the French galloped forward and began cutting down their own men.

More French men-at-arms arrived and formed up to charge the English lines, although most of the French army, which greatly outnumbered the English, was still pushing along the narrow forest road. As a result the entire French force was never able to engage at one time. Now the French made their fatal mistake. Instead of directing their attack against the English archers' outflanking wings, they drove straight for the center of the line and the English knights.

As the French knights trotted up the hill, picking their way among the bodies of Genoese bowmen, the English archers poured a hail of arrows into their ranks. Many found their marks in crevices in the knights' armor, but much more devastating was the slaughter of horses. As the French steeds fell, knight after knight was sent crashing to the ground. Utter confusion reigned. The deadly shafts winged down on French reinforcements, until at last their troops were so disorganized that they were easy prey for the knights of the English king, who rode down to dispatch them.

Thousands of French knights, the flower of their chivalry, fell in that battle, as well as more thousands of French foot soldiers and archers. The English losses were almost nil. It was a complete triumph for Edward III. Crécy caused great excitement among military leaders of Europe, and brought about a complete revamping of tactics everywhere; it was also the beginning of the end of the dominance of the armored knight.

C Test   The English Longbow
Finishing Time _____
WPM _____

1   The English longbow

   a. brought about a change in military tactics.

   b. was not very accurate.

   c. had a relatively short range.

   d. could not be handled by one man.

2   During the battle of Crécy

   a. a short rain ruined the plans of the English.

   b. the French suffered great losses.

   c. the English suffered great losses.

   d. the superiority of the armored knight was established.

3   The most devastating effect of the English arrows was the

   a. confusion that arose from the sound of the arrows.

   b. fear that was provoked by the sight of the arrows.

   c. piercing of armor.

   d. slaughter of horses.

4   In the battle of Crécy, the English had the advantage of

   a. more loyal support from their men.

   b. advance warning of the attack.

   c. greater familiarity with the terrain.

   d. none of the above.

5   In the battle of Crécy, the English longbow

   a. proved inferior to the French crossbow.

       b. was too heavy to permit accurate firing.

       c. led to victory for the English.

       d. is described by none of the above.

       CS = Total number correct _____ *× 20 =*   %

S&C Selection
Starting Time _____

FREUD

Freud's new book, *The Interpretation of Dreams*, generally considered one of the major and most influential works of our time, appeared at the end of 1899. The motto on the title page is a quotation from Vergil's *Aeneid* which, translated, means, "If I cannot stir the gods above, I will move the infernal regions."

Before Freud, the weight of scientific opinion held that dreams could not be interpreted or had no great significance beyond revealing certain physical states in the dreamer which somehow spilled over into consciousness. Freud asserted that dreams were a part of psychic life, being the life of the mind during sleep. Consequently they could be studied by psychological techniques and their often mysterious language in the form of symbols and images translated into meaning. No dream was meaningless. A diligent searcher into the meanings could gain a better knowledge of a patient's hidden problems and thereby be in a position to provide more intelligent treatment. He himself had successfully treated patients other doctors had despaired of, by interpreting the dream symbols and presenting their significance to the patient.

Basic to Freud's whole theory of dreams was his insistence that the content of dreams revealed a wish in the dreamer, even though the wish might be disguised as something not wanted; this usually occurred when the secret wish was so buried or repressed that a person could not face it in his dream.

Beneath the surface images of a dream lay deeper, more meaningful ones which the conscious part of the mind deliberately covered up or repressed like a censor deleting parts of a message. But, like a crafty writer who tries to get past the censor, the unconscious desires were cunning and insistent on expressing themselves, thus causing the common distortions so familiar in the dream process.

Frequently a person, who in daily life seemed devoted to members of the family, might dream of the death of a loved one, a sister clearly visualizing her brother in the tomb. How could such a dream be a wish fulfillment? Freud traced the dream back to childhood rivalry and resentments, and even hatred between siblings, that is, children of the same parents. At times of conflict, a brother or sister might wish that the other had not been born and want the troublesome rival to simply disappear. Since no desire, conscious or unconscious, remained completely lost in the psyche's deep reservoir, such childhood wishes could return in the grown person's dream. Children could also wish for the death of their parents. Men, Freud noticed, tended to dream of their father's death, women of their mother's. These dreams, too, stemmed from an earlier time, revealing the competitiveness even in little children for the chief place in the life of the parent of the opposite sex. The unconscious was amoral, indifferent to what society considered right or wrong, good or bad.

Dreams also provided wish fulfillment in more obvious ways. They were the guardians of sleep, welling up from the unconscious to provide the dreamer with imaginary satisfactions that were denied him in reality. A crippled person might dream of being a famous athlete, a coward of winning a medal for bravery, a poor man of being rich— demonstrating the truth underlying the common saying, "I couldn't have imagined anything better even in my wildest dreams."

Secret desires, not acceptable by a person's conscience or by conventional social standards, also found satisfaction in dreams. A woman who was normally prudish might dream of walking naked in a crowd without feeling any embarrassment. Such a dream, Freud theorized, was one of a state of childish innocence when there had been no embarrassment about being dandled by a nurse, mother or father in a naked state, or running about freely without the restriction of clothes. It was like a return to a paradise of the kind depicted in the story of Adam and Eve who also were without shame in their nakedness before they ate the fruit of the "tree of knowledge of good and evil" and so learned to be ashamed. Or, a stolid businessman with very correct ideas of behavior might dream of having a love relationship with someone other than his wife, someone he actually yearned for, but could not admit it to himself.

But how could nightmares fit into the pattern of dreams being guardians of sleep or the means of satisfying a wish? This did not change the dream's essential character, Freud said; it was only that the dream had failed to achieve its purpose. A nightmare or anxiety dream usually woke the sleeper before the repressed wish behind the dream could outwit the censor and come to complete fulfillment. It was as if a night watchman who was to protect the dreamer was forced to rouse him in order to ward off threatening danger. Although anxiety was the direct opposite of a wish, said Freud, the opposites lay very near to each other in association and actually coincided in the unconscious.

Freud recognized two main parts of every dream. The surface part of the dream, the most obvious and accessible, he called the manifest dream. Under or within that was the hidden or latent dream with its cargo of suggestion and symbol which could only be revealed by interpretation.

Much of Freud's book dealt with the symbols in dreams which after long study of myths, primitive rites, legends and history, he found to be mainly phallic, or sexual in origin. Some symbols, such as landscapes, ships, boxes, water, seemed always to represent the female gender. Towers, pipes, spears, snakes, stood for the male. Much of the dream material came out of infantile experiences. Symbols were disguises for a reality which the dreamer could not face easily, whether the reality involved sexual desires or other desires which conflicted with a person's good opinion of himself.

Freud's book marked the beginning of a new era, one that is often called the "Freudian Age." *The Interpretation of Dreams*, a monumental undertaking and a defiant one in the face of theories then held, is generally considered Freud's major work. But the majority of the professional critics derided the book when it appeared. One said it was no better than the cheap dream books found in cooks' pantries or in a gypsy fortuneteller's bag. Mostly, the book was ignored. It took eight years to sell the six hundred copies which were printed.

C Test Freud
Finishing Time _____
WPM _____

1 The selection deals with Freud's theory of

    a. sexual development.

    b. the racial unconscious.

    c. the interpretation of dreams.

    d. the functions of the superego.

2 Which of the following statements best describes Freud's theory of dreams?

    a. The symbols that appear in dreams are universal.

    b. Dreams basically express a wish of the dreamer.

    c. Most dreams are not subject to interpretation.

    d. Dreams are initiated by the physical discomforts of the dreamer.

3 According to Freud's theory, an adult who dreams of the death of a member of his family

    a. is self-destructive.

    b. is expressing fear of his own death.

    c. is expressing former childhood conflicts and wishes.

    d. suffers from neurotic anxiety.

4 The common expression, "I couldn't have imagined anything better even in my wildest dreams," illustrates the point that dreams

    a. provide satisfying wish fulfillments.

    b. are unpredictable.

    c. are based on creative impulses.

    d. reveal the regressive tendencies of the dreamer.

5 According to Freud, a nightmare

    a. expresses the death wish.

    b. has no symbolic content.

    c. is an expression of guilt.

    d. is described by none of the above.

6 The difference between the manifest dream and the latent dream is

    a. that the latent dream can only be revealed by interpretation.

    b. that the latent dream is based on guilt and shame.

    c. that the latent dream is obvious and accessible.

    d. none of the above.

7 Much of dream material

    a. is sexual in origin.

    b. arises from infantile experiences.

    c. involves the use of symbols.

    d. is described by all of the above.

CS = Total number correct _____ $\times$ *14.3 =*   %

S&C Selection
Starting Time _____

PALEOLITHIC MAN

By the use of all of these new technical devices, Upper Paleolithic man had acquired many advantages over his predecessors of the Lower and Middle periods. He could hunt more efficiently, in terms of both time and effort, and he could eat his food more quickly. The size of his communities was probably larger in most environments, and the time available for teaching and ceremonies longer. The archaeological record itself gives us some hints about his social structure, as it did with the earlier periods, but we no longer have to turn to living apes for ideas about how human beings may have got along together. Abundant evidence from the survivors of this ancient cultural level helps us piece out a broad picture.

The universe in which an individual lived consisted of himself, other people, the non-human part of the world which he perceived and experienced, and a host of symbols that had meaning to him in the way of life which he and his fellows led. The individual, having survived the rigors of outdoor life to the age of twenty-five, would be healthy and in good flesh, as zoo-keepers say: a highly efficient animal in its prime. Granting for a moment that this individual was a male, he undoubtedly had one or more wives and several children. He also had a number of brothers, sisters, and other close kin. Possibly a father or mother survived, but if so, that parent at the age of forty-five or fifty was considered old—in fact, was in the last stages of decrepitude. The total number of persons, mostly kin, whom our man habitually saw and dealt with was under fifty. Everyone whom he was used to seeing he knew; patterns of behavior had been so carefully worked out for thousands of years that he knew exactly what to do when his mother-in-law faced him on the path, or what cut of meat he should give his aging father to masticate between his worn and broken teeth. If he happened to see a stranger, he would take care.

If by some special kind of body paint or other telltale sign
he saw that the stranger was a member of a hostile group,
he would either kill the stranger or hide from him. The
choice of killing or hiding depended to a certain extent on
the place of the meeting. If it was on home territory and
the stranger seemed to be trespassing, particularly if he was
poaching game, then a spear-thrust would be the answer.
If our man was himself poaching, he would unquestionably
hide rather than take the offensive. If, however, the stranger
was painted in some special way—as for example to indicate
that he was bent on trade—or carried some sort of message
from one group to another, then our man would make himself
known to him, and a conversation would ensue, according
to polite procedure, either by speech alone, or by sign language if the two had no language in common.

Relations with the non-human world were frequent and
important. Animals, being more numerous than men, oc-
cupied man's attention. Day after day he hunted them, until
by the age of twenty-five he knew their habits intimately
and could even identify individual bears or wolves by their
tracks. He could tell if they were well or ill, glutted or
ravenous, old or young, male or female, pregnant or in milk.
He knew when the wolverine would climb a tree or the
bear decide to await him in a clump; many of his ancestors
and kin had been clawed or bitten to death by animals, and
these lessons had not been forgotten. Attention to animals
took as much of his time and energy as the work of any
man takes today. Hunting kept him away from camp for
days at a time and limited him to the companionship of
two or three other men, if indeed he did not hunt alone.

To the women the world of plants was almost equally
absorbing. From plants came roots and berries and succulent
leaves to piece out the menu, providing not only needed
nutritional factors, but also sustenance itself when the hunt
failed. From them came fuel to cook the meals and keep
the family warm. From them came fibers for baskets and
bags and cords and mats; from them also mysterious properties for curing sickness and easing pains. These properties
were attributed to spiritual beings who either lodged visibly
in the plants themselves or worked through their agency.
Burned wood became a substance of another kind—char-
coal—black paint. From the mineral world came iron oxide
to serve as red paint, and kaolin for white pigment. Flint,

too, was basic, and flint did not occur naturally in every part of the landscape. Those who had it could trade it, or let members of other tribes come through their territory to mine it. This kind of generosity paid off in that it allowed the members of several groups to meet one another, pass on ideas, and trade in other objects, like iron oxide or special kinds of wood. Only by such meetings could a new technique of flint-flaking be disseminated.

For still another reason it was good policy to carry on periodic relations with one's neighbors over the hill, particularly if the climate was changing or the annual rainfall variable. Suppose that a drought in the territory of band A drove most of the animals over into the land of B; then the A people would starve if they could not move. If they had seen the B people many times and danced and gone through ceremonies with them, perhaps their messenger would return with an invitation: "Come over and share the hunting with us."

Every year there are certain times when food is more abundant than at the other times. During these times of abundance, many people can live off a few square miles of land. That is the time when people can get together, when two or three hundred people, members of from two to a half-dozen bands, can meet. Each meeting of many persons needs an agenda; otherwise it becomes a disorganized mob, and conflict follows. The agendas of such meetings are time-honored and traditional. Older men talk together formally; younger men wrestle; at certain times designated individuals get up and dance, acting out routines derived from the behavior of certain animals, from the actions of hunters pursuing or stalking these animals, and other routines derived from famous deeds of ancestors long dead. At night, fires will glow on painted bodies and painted faces; formal dancing routines shift, and couples make for the shrubbery. Normal sexual rules break down, and only the basic tabus of mother and son, father and daughter, brother and sister, prevent nocturnal unions.

These meetings served a biological as well as a social purpose. Women whose sexual relations with their husbands had been fruitless were given another chance, which enhanced the survival value of all groups concerned. The exchange of genes was just as important as the trading of flint for special kinds of wood which went on under cover of ritual, for it aided the process of variation and selection essential to the perpetuation of all contributing communities. After these meetings formal marriages were also made between groups.

The group itself consisted of a small number of separate families of father, mother, and children; two generations were normally represented, and sometimes three, but few individuals lived past their physiological prime. Generations in themselves were not important. A man forty may have a brother twenty. A woman may have a daughter and a sister of the same age. Age was more important, because persons of the same age and sex did the same things, and did them together.

These age groups were designated by different symbols, in the style of clothing, in manner of using body paint, or in behavior itself. The repertory of symbols used by the members of a band was complete; it represented all of the possible relationships among people and between human beings and the inhuman, or superhuman, world. First of all is the configuration of language. We do not know what languages the hunters of the Late Pleistocene spoke, but we may be sure they were numerous. Simple hunters living today have almost as many languages as there are groups of bands which come together for ceremonies in the fat seasons. We may be equally sure that they were adequate, in that every kind of animal hunted had a whole roster of names to indicate its sex, age, and condition; that if snow was important, a dozen or more words would designate snow, while the list of numbers may have gone from three or six to "many," *i.e.,* infinity.

Other symbols expressed the relationship of man to nature. Each category of useful beast or herb had its soul, which presented itself from time to time to people, giving men important messages. Game laws and laws of conservation were rigidly enforced by a system of tabus which automatically protected important species at certain seasons, through the fear of vengeance from the spirits concerned. These spirits could also be invoked for success in hunting, by the hunters acting out an event in the mythological creation of a certain kind of animal. Above all, the equilibrium of nature in which man participates must not be disturbed; ceremonies symbolically maintain it, making it clear that for a man to kill a deer is a part of the normal course of natural events in the environment in which he lives.

The world of the hunter cannot be limited to the part

of the far-stretching landscape on which he pursues his game, to the members of his own group and those of his friends and enemies over the hills, the animals and plants that sustain his life, and the spirits of these animals and plants. It must also include the spirits of his own ancestors, who, though they are dead, are still in a sense alive. The length of time that the soul of a dead man survives depends on his importance to those who are still alive. If he was a fine hunter in his prime, the leader of the band, the man who divided the meat, the arbiter of quarrels, the teacher of boys, and a good husband, his death will cause a disturbance in the life of the band which will bring his image often to mind among most of its members. He is certainly finite and close at hand: he can be prayed to, invoked, asked for decisions in matters like those which he was accustomed to settle.

If he was an indifferent hunter, a poor husband, and a quarrelsome person, his soul will be dim, and before many years have passed people will forget about him. His soul will have disappeared. After many years have passed and no one still lives who has actually seen the great man whose soul was large after death, his exploits gradually become merged with those of still greater heroes of the past, whose name his own may supplant. Gradually the invisible world becomes peopled with a stable cast. These are the men and women who made the landscape, who caused this hill to rise and that brook to flow; some of them symbolize areas of disturbance between men and women, young and old, people and nature. Of the last, of course, the chief ones are the weather; storms may be caused by the anger of some great spirit unwittingly annoyed by human beings who have done something that disturbs the relationships within the group.

C Test   Paleolithic Man

Finishing Time _____

WPM _____

---

1 Paleolithic man was likely to

    a. deal habitually with over 200 persons.

    b. survive only to the age of about twenty.

    c. be unable to track bears or wolves.

    d. attack a member of a hostile group if the meeting was on home territory.

2 Paleolithic life was characterized by

    a. a great dependence upon hunting animals for food.

    b. a lack of family structure.

    c. loosely defined patterns of behavior between individuals.

    d. a great fear of animals.

3 The meetings of members of several bands were useful because they led to

    a. exchange of new remedies for illnesses.

    b. invasions of neighboring territories and expansion of land holdings.

    c. marriage between members of different bands.

    d. revitalization of religious customs.

4 The men of Paleolithic time probably

    a. did not have a spoken language.

    b. had no belief in spirits.

    c. were uninterested in the interactions of man and nature.

    d. used a system of symbols and language.

5 Which of the following statements describes the relationships between members of different bands?

    a. There was no overt hostility between members of different bands.

    b. Trade occurred between members of different bands.

    c. Trade occurred only between members of the same band.

    d. Food was never shared with members of a different band.

6 Paleolithic men

    a. were very poor hunters.

    b. knew the habits of animals very well.

    c. were very poor fishermen.

    d. made no use of plant life for food.

7   The spiritual life of Paleolithic man included the belief

    a. that animals and plants had souls.

    b. that ancestors had souls.

    c. that changes in weather were caused by spirits.

    d. in all of the above.

CS = Total number correct _____ × *14.3 =*   %

S&C Selection

Starting Time _____

THE COMING CRISIS IN EDUCATION

According to the U.S. Office of Education, total enrollments in all schools and colleges may reach 60,000,000 in 1970. Little wonder there is a rush to bring automation into the classroom!

The Secondary Schools

By 1970 high-school buildings will be bursting, because there will be three students for every two students they had ten years before. Grade schools will have a short chance to catch their breath until the middle 1970's when the next big wave of pupils begins to press into the classrooms.

Traditional methods of grouping and teaching children will be discarded in order to meet changed conditions. For instance, it has been estimated that one out of every five boys and girls entering first grade will be able to read. Many three-year-olds will be reading first-grade books, thanks to the "talking typewriter" which prints a large letter and names its sound on a speaker when the child pushes a key. Such youngsters will be ready for third- or fourth-grade work when they enter school.

Experiments conducted during the early 1960's showed that children as young as two may benefit greatly from special schooling designed to meet the abilities of their young minds. Some youngsters will be starting their formal education long before they are five or six.

Secondary education as we knew it in the 1950's and 1960's will be quite different by 1975. The tremendous increase in the number of students and the continued shortage of teachers will make it necessary to adopt new teaching methods. Some grade-school and high-school students will spend as much as 30 per cent of their classroom time learning from special films and live television programs. Electronic-language laboratories, training simulators—that give the "feel" of an automobile and the "look" of a road to the student driver, animated displays and electronic information centers will be widely used. Teaching machines that bear little resemblance to those introduced in the early 1960's will be used widely, as will *programed instruction*.

Programed Instruction

One of the latest developments in education is called programed instruction. This refers to a course of study in any subject which takes the place of a tutor. The course may be offered by a machine or a textbook. Each pupil studies alone and works on material that is presented in short sections; the student advances as quickly or as slowly as he desires, his progress depending upon his ability and application. The program is usually a series of queries or statements which the student must read, after which he is asked to reply to questions by filling in a blank, solving a problem or choosing one of several answers.

Programed instruction is just one educational device which teachers will use to help them do a better job. It will not replace instructors but it will help partially to make up for the teacher shortage and enable faculty members to spend more time on individual instruction. During the years ahead, much research will be undertaken to improve and expand the various teaching methods. The principles of programed instruction will be applied to teaching methods such as television, textbooks, films and other audio-visual materials, workbooks, class teaching and group study.

It is quite probable that programed instruction will put an end to the time-honored institution of cheating on examinations! Machines will be made so foolproof that those who have to resort to writing on their fingernails, peeking at notes or copying from the next person in order to pass a course, will be urged to seek better employment for their talents outside school!

New Courses

By 1970 there will be a strong demand for many new courses to meet the needs of a changing world. For example: The increased use of computers and the growing importance of mathematics will require many students to take subjects such as number progressions, the duodecimal system, binary systems and number theory.

To meet our nation's requirements for more trained scientists so that we can compete successfully with other countries, chemistry, mathematics and physics will become basic courses in most high-school programs.

Methods of teaching science will continue to change and improve. Students will no longer have to learn tables and formulas by rote. Instead, they will be encouraged to concentrate on observing, thinking and working out their own conclusions.

A knowledge of foreign languages will become more important as the world continues to shrink. Chinese, Japanese, Russian and the many tongues of other Asian and African countries will be taught in numerous places. Language instruction will start in the fourth grade instead of waiting until pupils enter junior or senior high school. Another year of high-school education will be available for those who do not plan to enter a two- or four-year college.

Teaching jobs will always be plentiful. By 1970 we shall need almost 2,200,000 teachers in our elementary and secondary schools. Colleges and universities will also be seeking a multitude of instructors to teach in their expanded facilities.

Tomorrow's Colleges

When the expected 9,000,000 young men and women report to colleges for classes in the early 1970's, the student will find here, too, that television plays an important role. He will spend many hours in large lecture halls watching television educational films and hearing lectures taped by prominent scholars and educators. He will study much of the time in a carrel equipped with a small television screen and audio system. From here he will be able to dial into the library "resource center" which will contain magnetic tape recordings of information on all subjects. The carrel will also contain a teaching machine. When the student is ready to give his answers to various questions, he will register his responses on a central computer by pushing buttons. Thus he will make a record of his learning progress available for the college teaching staff to review. Small seminars and counseling sessions will replace the usual classes.

Although many educators disapprove of such plans, these innovations will be necessary in most institutions because this is the only way a college education can be provided for the increased number of students who will apply for admission. There simply will not be enough teachers or classrooms to offer the kind of instruction that has always been available on most campuses. Nevertheless, there will be some compensation for this mechanized teaching system. An important part of the education process for each individual is the chance to exchange ideas, defend a position and test opinions on others. This should be possible through participation in formal or informal student discussion groups led at times by members of the faculty.

One important reason for the huge anticipated rise in college enrollments is the growing emphasis that will be placed on education. A four-year college course will no longer suffice in an increasing number of fields. Another factor that will compel young people to continue their education after high school will be the difficulty of finding jobs in occupations that call for little or no skills. Therefore, the wise high-school graduate will obtain training in a technical school or a university in order to qualify for a position.

Something for Everyone

The two-year college may well act as a safety valve in the coming education crisis. It is expected that high schools will offer postgraduate courses for those anxious to learn a skill that does not require a college background. However, a large number of young people will seek positions that call for more education than can be obtained at high school but not as much as is offered at the four-year undergraduate college. Such job opportunities will be found in engineering, technical work, merchandising, automobile mechanics, electronic computer operation and maintenance, service industries and similar fields.

To enable high-school graduates to qualify for openings in these occupations, more and more two-year colleges and technical institutions will be established and offer associate degrees. The greater number of these schools will be the so-called "community colleges." Unlike some 275 independent private junior colleges, they are supported by taxes and controlled by the local school or junior college district, a city, county or state. Such schools are inexpensive to attend, some are free. Thus, those who cannot afford to attend a four-year college can at least obtain a two-year education and in certain instances may transfer to a four-year institution to earn a B.A. or B.S. degree.

C Test   The Coming Crisis in Education
Finishing Time _____
WPM _____

---

1 Programed instruction refers to a course of study that

    a. takes the place of a teacher.

    b. is offered by a machine or a textbook.

    c. allows the student to advance at his own speed.

    d. is described by all of the above.

2 In programed instruction, the student

    a. is given a series of questions or statements.

    b. may be asked to reply to questions.

    c. may be asked to solve a problem.

    d. experiences all of the above.

3 Programed instruction

    a. is likely to be discarded because it encourages cheating.

    b. may put an end to cheating.

    c. will decrease individual instruction.

    d. is described by none of the above.

4 Televised educational films

    a. are not realistic enough to provide a challenging educational experience.

    b. will be replaced by teaching machines.

    c. will be used with increasing frequency.

    d. are already outmoded.

5   The two-year college

    a. may act as a "safety valve" in the coming education crisis.
    b. will increase the problems of overcrowding at the college level.
    c. will be replaced entirely by small, four-year liberal arts colleges.
    d. will suffer a loss in enrollment because of high tuition rates.

6   Programed instruction may help to solve the problem created by

    a. students' declining interest in mathematics and the physical sciences.
    b. the increasing enrollment in grade schools, high schools, and colleges.
    c. the poor training of technical staff in government offices.
    d. the poor training of administrative staff in government offices.

CS = Total number correct _____ × *16.6 =*   %

Speed Test

Starting Time _____

ANTHROPOLOGY AS SCIENCE AND SCHOLARSHIP

The kind of people who make good anthropologists could have put their abilities to use in many other professions. In the past, a number of anthropologists—Franz Boas, George Bird Grinnell, Ruth Benedict, to name only a few—came into anthropology from other fields. Today more students may come directly into this field. But no single ability or talent is by itself a crucial one.

Although anthropology is a research science, it offers limited opportunities for the "armchair" scholar whose chief area of activities is bounded by library walls. Instead, an anthropologist may spend a great deal of time out-of-doors, living under primitive conditions, very much as an explorer, a prospector, a geologist, or an oil engineer may have to do. Because anthropology means working with people, learning languages is a necessary skill—not merely learning to recognize the written form of another language, as students often do in modern language classes (a kind of learning that may carry them through some other sciences), but learning them as a living form of speech, heard and spoken. Our American methods of teaching often fail a student in this, but the student who decides to be an anthropologist must learn how to learn spoken versions of languages—including those he may be the first to record in written form.

Anthropology takes a lot of hard thinking. But there are many things that have to be done with one's hands—typing notes, sorting and packing and cataloguing specimens, running a tape recorder, taking photographs and developing them. Besides, it is necessary to describe what other people do with their hands—weaving and carving, throwing spears, building houses and canoes, tying knots, making pottery, planting and harvesting crops, cooking and making clothes, fishing and sailing boats. It is difficult to describe accurately all the techniques in which people use their hands unless you are good at using your own and can get a sense of what they are doing.

Above all, anthropology means getting along with people—not just a few close friends and relatives, but all kinds of people—including the intelligent and the stupid, men and women, the friendly and the bad-tempered, people in high positions and the village ne'er-do-well, sharp traders, the sick and the handicapped as well as healthy people, skilled craftsmen, and dedicated artists. It means having a memory for people and learning to remember who and what they are, in the way that a good politician must, not only recognizing their faces and knowing their names but also keeping in mind details of the things that are important about them. And, almost always, anthropologists need to have a real concern for human beings; they must care about what is happening in their village and tribe and what is happening in the world. An anthropologist who has little feeling for people finds fieldwork too trying and soon gives it up.

Field anthropology involves taking an interest in the arts, having a feeling for the designs people make, the myths they tell, the songs they sing, and their dramatic performances. Very often students are attracted to anthropology through some first acquaintance with an Indian dance, a piece of exotic music, or a collection of folk songs out of our own past. But even those students who are not especially attracted to the arts will find it necessary to know something about them. Not very many will have the kind of talent that Melville Herskovits, for example, had for learning the intricate patterns of African drumming, so that he could play together with the more expert of his informants. But enough interest and ability to understand is necessary so that talking with an expert is enjoyable to both of them. Of course, students who are already interested in the arts will have to make a choice among the various ones in which anthropologists specialize in order to develop this interest into a first-rate skill.

Anthropologists also must understand and care about good scholarship. They must know how to work with old documents, unpublished government reports, musty, crumbling records of old explorations, diaries and surveyors' maps, tax records, parish records and local censuses, and missionaries' accounts of the "cruel and barbarous behavior" of the people they came to convert. It may be necessary, for research purposes, to learn an archaic form of a language—medieval Latin or Old Icelandic. Or it may be necessary to classify records written in Spanish describing the Southwest before this region became part of the United States. Or research may combine a study of nineteenth-century New England tombstones with an analysis of the records of the religious thought of the period, as in a project James Deetz of the University of California at Santa Barbara has been working on.

Clearly, while anthropologists cannot be "armchair" scholars, they also cannot be the kind of people (as some journalists and psychiatrists are) who only enjoy working with people and find work with books a deadly bore. Essentially, anthropologists are people who enjoy the discovery of living culture in all its diversity, whether research takes the form of discovery of the distant past, through the evidence of the bones of very early men, or a find of flaked-stone tools, or the crumbling outlines of an ancient, long-buried city; whether an old culture emerges from an investigation into the early forms of government in Iceland through a search of old records and traditional tales or from a study of the correspondence and records and orders of fur trading companies in their relations with the Indians to whom they sold guns and traps; or whether research takes the multiple forms of modern fieldwork. On the balance, an anthropologist will develop most fully the skills he needs to work on the problems and the areas of his special choice. But what holds anthropologists together is their common interest in living cultures, old and new.

Some of their ways of thinking and working tie them very closely to the natural sciences. Anthropologists must understand how to approach a problem scientifically, that is, how to establish hypotheses that can be tested, retested, and revised in the light of new evidence. For their work they need to draw now on one natural science and now on another—geology, botany, physiology, anatomy, ornithology, physics, and chemistry. One cannot always predict which body of scientific information it will be necessary to tap for the solution of some problem. The archeologist digging in a kitchen midden (an ancient rubbish heap) and the ethnologist working with the modern people whose village is built close by, perhaps even on top of, the archeologist's site, may try to establish a link between past and present through an analysis of food particles or a combined analysis of old pottery sherds and modern pottery-making techniques. Whatever their problem, anthropologists must understand science as a way of thinking and carrying out investigations, and they must know enough about other sciences both to ask meaningful questions and to make use of the information other scientists can supply.

Finishing Time _____
WPM _____

Pre-Reading

8

The purpose for which you are reading will naturally influence many aspects of the way in which you read. Certain materials will be read slowly and carefully with great attention to detail. Other types of material will be gone over lightly. If you are going to curl up with a detective story, chances are that your purpose in reading is relaxation and entertainment. If you are reading something in connection with your work, you are probably gathering important information for the conduct of your job. Your level of attention to detail differs in these two situations. You may not make a conscious decision to change the way in which you read, though it is a fact that reading rate and attention vary a great deal from one type of material to another. Such variation can be very useful if it is applied appropriately. The techniques of pre-reading that are described in this chapter are aimed at maximizing the extent to which time can be saved, on the one hand, and information well understood, on the other.

It has been found that a person who knows the general "gist" of an article before he begins a thorough reading is able to master the content much more rapidly than a person who does not. Articles that are preceded by an abstract are usually better understood on first reading than articles that are not. Pre-reading is essentially a technique for making an abstract for oneself before beginning a thorough reading of an article or book.

The type of pre-reading that you employ will depend upon your main purposes in reading a particular article or book. If you are, for example, browsing in the library looking for some information about a specific subject, pre-reading can be used to discover whether or not a particular book contains the right kind of information. Is the book too advanced or too elementary? Does the author deal with the aspects of the subject that interest you? Or you might be reading material that has been recommended by your teacher or employer. If your grade or job depends to some extent on how well you master the pertinent materials, you will probably want to be sure of understanding the reading material very thoroughly. Techniques of pre-reading can, therefore, be used to facilitate your understanding and retention of the materials that you read.

Pre-Reading an Article

Articles in conventional English nonfiction writing usually have an introduction, a body, and a conclusion. Furthermore, each paragraph has a "topic sentence," that is, a sentence that expresses the main content of the paragraph. The first or second sentence in the paragraph is usually, although not invariably, the topic sentence. By reading the first paragraph of an article, the first two sentences of each succeeding paragraph, and the last paragraph in its entirety, you will provide yourself with an outline of the article that can be quite useful to have before thoroughly reading the entire article. On the basis of the pre-reading you will have a general idea of the content and purpose of the article. Your own interest in the subject and the importance of the information can be used as guides in setting the level of speed and attention to detail that you will apply to reading the entire article. Furthermore, the pre-reading, by familiarizing you with the general content of the article, will enable you to grasp the main ideas more rapidly during the thorough reading. On the other hand, a pre-reading may indicate that a reading of the entire article is not necessary for your purposes.

Pre-Reading a Book

The techniques of pre-reading described in this section apply only to nonfiction books. Most nonfiction books, as part of their formal structure, contain many supplementary aids to reading and understanding the text. With the exception of the index, which most people use on occasion, supplementary aids are used too infrequently by most readers. In addition to the actual text, books often have a preface, a table of contents, an introductory section, an index, a glossary, and appendices that include supplementary information to the text.

The index will often prove useful when you are looking for a specific item of information. Instead of thumbing through the entire book, turn immediately to the index where topic headings are arranged alphabetically. Look up the key words as well as synonyms for the subject matter you wish to find. You can turn to the pages indicated and determine at once if the desired information is provided.

Usually you will have some purpose in mind when you are selecting a book. In the section of the library or bookstore that contains books on the subject matter in which you are interested, you may find a large selection of books. You may be able to eliminate some of these books by looking at their titles, others by their dates of publication. If you are looking, for example, for a book that deals with the most recent developments in undersea exploration, you will not select a book that was published fifteen years ago. On the other hand, your problem may be less easily solved. You might be confronted with eight books of recent date, all of whose titles look equally promising. There are several simple ways of determining which of these books would be best suited to your purpose. Open to the preface or introduction and find out what the author's purpose was in writing the book. The author will generally indicate the boundaries of the subject matter with which the book deals. The preface and the table of contents can be skimmed for this information in a few minutes.

Suppose you have selected the book that seems to deal most completely with those aspects of the subject that interest you. How can you obtain the most information from the book in an efficient manner? Reread the table of contents in order to get a picture of the overall organization of the book. If you are aware of the nature and location of information that is provided in the text and appendices, you are more likely to make use of this information when you are reading the book. Too many students make no attempt to grasp the organization of a book before they read it, and they ignore supplementary material. Simple use of the index, glossary, and appendices will often clear up questions that arise during reading.

Books are divided into chapters, and headings and subheadings are often found within each chapter. Take advantage of these divisions to provide yourself with an outline of the book, as you did with topic sentences in articles. Certain parts of the book are likely to be more important to you than others. Begin a book by reading the chapter titles and the headings within chapters. In this way you will be able to locate the most important sections for your purpose. You will not have to read an entire section before you find out that it is really not germane. In fact, you may be able to obtain sufficient information from many sections of the book with no more than a pre-reading. If a book is divided into chapters or sections, it is a good idea to pre-read each section as if it were an article. If the chapters are long enough to discourage reading of the topic sentence in each paragraph, then simply read the first and last paragraph of each chapter. You will be surprised to find that your understanding is greatly enhanced when you provide yourself with an overview before you read a book. In addition, if you are seeking specific information, you will save yourself a great deal of time by using the foregoing techniques to locate the information.

Concluding Remarks

You will find that your capacities for rapid reading will continue to improve as the methods you have learned become second nature to you. As has been emphasized throughout this guide, the best way to maintain the techniques is by deliberate practice until the habits are completely automatic.

Besides having finished the exercises provided in the guide, also allow your everyday reading to serve as exercise material. Treat all of your newspaper reading, for example, as column reading and eliminate left-to-right eye movements. Pay close attention to the ways in which your eyes move and guard against slipping back into former line-by-line habits.

With books and magazines, eventually you need not use your hand as a guide for the S-pattern. Your eyes will move across and down the page simultaneously without the assistance of your hand. Each individual is his own best judge of the appropriate point for eliminating hand-eye coordination. Be cautioned against eliminating the guide too soon, for you may tend to return to old reading habits. Wait until you are sure that the S-pattern is occurring automatically without your consciously thinking about it. When this point is reached, you may safely eliminate the use of a guide.

In effect, you have learned an extremely efficient means of doing something that you already knew how to do: read. You have eliminated habits that interfere with the rapid intake of words from the page. The crucial abilities for accomplishing this task reside in your previous knowledge and experience with the English language; without the appropriate motor habits, however, these abilities cannot be fully utilized. Be careful to exercise and maintain the new reading habits. You will be amply rewarded by the ease with which you read and comprehend written material of every kind.

Additional
S&C Selections
and Speed Tests

S&C Selection

Starting Time _____

THE TRAGIC CHASE

The New Year of 1948 was only a week old—the second
year of the Disk Era—when death took his first toll. Before,
however, that sad and baffling tale is plotted out, let us
remember one thing of great importance. These "tres-
passers"—if we should so call them—have been meticulously
careful "to observe the amenities." They have always kept
their distance, kept out of the way and when they have found
that they have strayed onto our unmarked air traffic lanes
have at once cleared off. They may have been observing
us—or even may be interested in something other than us—but
certainly they have not pressed their curiosity to any imper-
tinent lengths. There is no evidence that they have ever
made any motion toward landing. Though one or two not
very good reports say they did come near the ground, they
certainly took care to do so when no one was about who
might object. We must repeat, they have always tried to
get out of the way.

For it is of the utmost importance we should never forget
that. And it is of the utmost importance that we should
remember that fact when we are reading this chapter. For
terrible as the encounter proved, the "encountered," the
visitor, *did everything, within its remarkable powers, to avoid
a contact, to keep clear of complications.* Though as terrible
a monster as any the human eye has ever rested on, it ran
like a hare away from the rash man who pursued it. That
being clear beyond a doubt, now we must have the story.

It is also clear beyond a doubt that the authorities were
uneasy. Of course they were or they would be unfit to be
authorities. They were caught between two concerns, two
acute anxieties. The first thing was of course, "What the
Devil is this?" No one is inspired today and everyone knows
it. Today the more informed you are, the better you know
that your best and brightest guess peers over the edge of

a blank, black abyss, out of which no one knows what next will emerge.

The second concern that a lively authority in this up-to-date, going-to-pieces world knows is that no one knows what the public will stand. What if the wildest fear proved true? What if the last thing we are clinging to in the back of our minds—that (though God and inspired prophets and infallible authorities are all put by public opinion under a cloud) at least Man is the one thing that matters, at least we are the one person who can think and act and direct our fate—what if that is untrue? What if there are other creatures as clever, yes, much more clever than we? Now, would the public—the democratic, "I am the crown of creation and the master of my destiny," present-day public—stand for that view being squashed, flattened? Again nobody knows; and that question, of course, is second to none to a democratic politician.

So the authorities have been uneasy and have tried, like all uneasy people in control, to keep a straight face and say as little as possible. But they had to find out. It was on the seventh of January, 1948, that the New Year brought as a present the possibility of finding out. And the offer was a big one—the biggest ever up to date.

Fort Knox in Kentucky (famous throughout the world as the place where the vastest heap of gold ever accumulated in the history of man used to be kept buried) was chosen as the center of the scene of action—and tragedy. This was to be no case where somewhere off the track, over some quiet countryside, in the night, a couple or maybe one observer saw something for a few moments. No, it was to be (as far as the word "showing" means showing something) a showdown. It was just getting on for three in the afternoon—the time when the light is still very good and men fresh and alert. The State Police had been the first to give the warning about half-past two. Certainly scores of people had already reported seeing something that made the State Police call to the Military Police as a matter of immediate need.

A very big object that shone brightly in the afternoon light was traveling through the sky at a vast speed. And it was evidently making its way toward a big Air Force Field, the Goodman Base. The Air Field was then on the alert.

And those on watch didn't have to wait long. The Goodman Field tower was manned with its leading personnel. The Commanding Officer, Colonel Hix, was in control there. He was using his binoculars and they had found their mark. The clouds were broken. Through them had appeared something which made the warnings sent ahead seem anything but exaggerated. The clouds thinned and the whole group of expert and responsible people—as competent a bunch as could be found in all the world—the entire team, saw. It was huge. The size must be estimated. There wasn't much doubt about it—only that it couldn't be! But any estimate which was made by ordinary checking seemed to show that it must be, say at the least, five hundred feet across! What there was no doubt about (and this was a new saucer style)—it shot out in the daylight pulses or blasts of red flame.

But the group in the tower weren't, of course, just going to stand and gape and hope the clouds would clear off and the "thing" oblige by standing still. It was clearly going its own sweet way at its own strong gallop. So, not expecting otherwise, the Command had made ready. Three fighting planes were already up and racing every moment higher to come up with the intruder. Nor had the command to wait.

One of the most wonderful features of modern flying, and what has made for so much of its security, is that the ground controls and commands and the ships in the sky can keep in constant touch, in instant exchange, with each other. And now the scouts hidden high above the clouds began to speak clearly to the whole group in the tower. At least the man in command of the scout fleet of three was now speaking. That was Captain James Mantell.

His report was good insofar as it was not disappointing. But it was grim too. Yes, he had the quarry in view. He was on its tracks. And there had been no exaggeration. It was of "tremendous size." It looked, too, as though it were metallic.

Then the voice from the far-up plane went on. "The thing is climbing." The next phrase was hopeful. "It's going only half the speed of the pursuit." Yes, he'd try to close in. But after five minutes when the loudspeaker again took up its tale it was not so certain. The monster had evidently taken fright.   It had shown its mettle—it was now climbing at close on 400 mph.

When the speaker again addressed the tower group the voice was from one of Mantell's companions.   Both he and his fellow plane had seen the object.   But they had lost sight of it now and of Mantell.   For he had gone on up after it and had disappeared in still higher clouds.

At last, at quarter past three, Mantell's voice was heard again.   He was holding on and up.   But the thing was still rising above him and maybe increasing the gap between them.   Still he'd track it as far as he could go—he thought he could stand up to 20,000 altitude.   Then if that didn't bring him at least to a better view and closer up, he'd give over.

Probably he did.   No one knows for certain.   What did show up was dumb, dead dumb.   The wreckage of his plane was picked up over a wide area.   How he actually met his death no one could say for sure—but dead he was. When his voice could no longer be got on the loudspeaker, the Command ordered one of his companions to search upward.   Taking oxygen apparatus, he not only went to 33,000 feet.   He swung over hundreds of miles of skyscape. But there was not a glimmer of the immense thing they had all seen rolling above them.

Fort Knox made a release on the subject.   The Commander, Colonel Hix, was allowed to have watched the visitor, which was said to be "unidentified," and Captain Mantell was declared as killed while chasing it.   "The rest," as a famous and inconclusive play concludes by saying, "is silence."   But there was a rumor that at Columbus, Ohio, at the airfield there, as the sun was setting on that fatal day, a disk rushed overhead and that this disk had a big flaming flue-blast trailing out behind it.

So the tragic chase closed with the first saucer casualty. The sacrifice made by the gallant pioneer didn't add to our knowledge anything more than might have been gleaned from the ground.   The observations from the tower showed that it was a new species and maybe a new genus of this strange visitation.   Before, no disk of that size had been noted—though some may have been as big, but too high to be gauged.   But what none before had shown was this great flare of angry incandescence from the stern.

And still there were more to come—to make the whole problem more of a headache—more facts to make the whole thing more incredible, less able to be fitted into any, even the most unpleasant of, human explanations. Further, as we shall see in the next chapter, with unabated courage, pilots were ready to try and tackle and maybe intercept one of these uninvited visitors.

C Test   The Tragic Chase
Finishing Time _____
WPM _____

---

1 There is evidence that flying saucers

   a. are controlled by superintelligent beings.
   b. are propelled by atomic energy.
   c. try to land on earth.
   d. try to keep out of the way.

2 The chase that is described in this selection was tragic because

   a. many people were burned in blasts of heat that came from the object.
   b. one man was killed while chasing the object.
   c. five men were killed in pursuit of the object.
   d. the research efforts of a team had been totally wasted.

3 The center of the scene of action for the chase of the flying object was

   a. Fort Knox, Kentucky.
   b. Washington, D.C.
   c. New York City.
   d. the great plains.

4 The most notable of the object's physical characteristics were its size and

   a. means of locomotion.
   b. silvery sheen.
   c. blasts of flame.
   d. sound.

5 Captain James Mantell died chasing the object. The wreckage from his plane indicated that the crash was caused by

    a. flames from the object.

    b. instrument failure in his plane.

    c. his loss of consciousness.

    d. unknown factors.

CS = Total number correct _____ × *20 =*   %

S&C Selection

Starting Time _____

BEAVER CUTTING

Beavers are highly important to the ecology of the north. Their ponds provide habitat for black mallards and wood ducks, forage and refuge from flies for deer and moose. Flowages and dams act as flood controls and water storage, and foresters depend on them during fires as barriers against the flames.

Trout fishermen are divided in their opinions. Some say that streams are improved because back of every dam is a pool. Others bemoan the fact that dams eliminate fast water, all the ripples and natural swirls that harbor trout, and that eventually all trees beside a stream are either cut by beavers or killed by their flooding.

The fact that an adult beaver might down as many as a hundred trees in a year shows what damage to forest cover can take place, explains why colonies are doomed almost as soon as they are established because of the vast quantities of food they need. After a few years all trees within reach are gone, including stands at the far ends of canals leading from the ponds. Then the colony must move to an untouched area, to return only when new growth has come back around the homes they have abandoned.

While they have enemies—wolves, coyotes, and bobcats, and in the old days the wolverine—because of the nature of their habitat they have little to fear. Nothing can touch them all winter long while their houses are frozen solid, nor during the summer if they stay close enough to water. Their greatest enemies are disease and lack of food. When fires are kept under control and the pine and spruce grow tall, the beavers face their end. Only when aspen and birch come in do they thrive for long, and so it must have been in the early days. Tremendous fires between the stands of virgin pine produced their breeding-grounds, and when these were exhausted the trade declined.

I examined the fresh cutting, the little pile of white chips that lay around the base of the stump, the peeled branch that lay silvery white in the water just offshore. Across the channel to the west was a colony I knew, one of hundreds that now dot the canoe country. It was high time I visited the beavers again, and now I had a visit to return. I paddled across the bay and, at the mouth of a creek coming down from the northwest, beached the canoe and hiked upstream until I came to the dam. It was late when I got there, and the water lay like a pool of wine among the birches. The house rose in conical splendor in the very center of the pond, the dam curving smoothly against the flow. Though it was not large, generations of beavers had worked there building this wilderness bridge across the creek. From its mud-encrusted walls came a constant trickling, the overflow from the pond above. The water was high and into the trees, and dead birches stood knee deep around the edges. They stood there white and broken and ghostlike against the wall of black spruces behind them.

I thought as I sat there of the tremendous dam on Longstaff Creek to the south. It is very old, and no beavers have been there for many years. A quarter of a mile in length, it is wide enough on top for a team of horses and a sleigh, and the grassy meadow above is over a mile across. That dam was of the past, dated from the days of Radisson and Groseilliers. The meadow with its black rich soil might someday make a farm, but now it lies unused with the little creek winding lazily through it on its way to the lake.

To make the beavers work on the dam below me, I broke through its crest, tore out several poplar sticks and stones and kicked away the mud. Soon the water surged noisily through the gap, a challenge the beavers could not ignore.

I climbed the hillside then and settled down to wait. Perhaps they might cut some aspen right before me, drag the branches to the dam, and carry armfuls of mud to hold them down. Suddenly a head showed near the break and a beaver climbed out and made a survey. Soon there were others, and then I heard the sound of a tree being felled. I could not see, for it was dusk, but there was a swish, and a small tree fell to the ground; more gnawing and beavers were swimming toward the break with branches held firmly in their teeth. Up into the gap they went, then, with great splashing and commotion, dove below for mud. After a while there was no further sound of rushing water, and I could hear the beavers swimming and working their way up the canals toward the aspen grove and coming back again to the storage pile beside the house.

As I sat there on the hillside watching the changing color in the pool, my notebook was forgotten and I was conscious only of the wild and placid beauty of the scene below. Such scenes had taken place before Columbus ever dreamed of a new continent. Here was primitive America, and in this little valley there had been no change. While the continent had been tamed and harnessed to the will of man, here time stood still.

C Test Beaver Cutting

Finishing Time _____

WPM _____

---

1 According to trout fishermen

    a. beaver dams improve streams because they create pools.

    b. beaver dams are damaging because they eliminate the fast water and natural swirls that harbor trout.

    c. as a result of the beavers' activity, all of the trees beside a stream are eventually cut down or flooded out.

    d. all of the above are true.

2 Beaver colonies are doomed almost as soon as they are established because of the

    a. vast quantities of food that they need.

    b. great number of natural enemies that they have.

    c. large amount of in-group fighting.

    d. waste-product contamination of streams and rivers.

3 The author made a break in the dam

    a. as the result of an accidental fall.

b. in order to increase his catch of trout.

c. in order to observe the beavers repair the break.

d. for none of the above reasons.

4 After the break in the dam was made the

a. beavers ignored it.

b. rushing water enlarged the break.

c. beavers felled trees and repaired the dam.

d. author went on his way.

CS = Total number correct _____ × *25 =*   %

S&C Selection

Starting Time _____

THE SPAWNING

It was February and the mercury was down to twenty below zero. We took off from the cabin when the moon was high and the surface of the lake glittering in its shine. The snow was firm, and the skis hissed as we pushed along. We did not stop to look at the moon or the stars, were only conscious of the fact we were moving through a brittle icy brightness, that the stars were close, almost close enough to touch. It was one of those winter nights in the north, one of those times close to midnight that come only when it is still and the moon is full.

We were off on important business, far more important than just going for a ski or enjoying the night. We were out to watch a spawning in midwinter, the mating of the eelpout, those brown eel-like deep-water fish that thrive in the cold depths of northern lakes. Seldom is one ever taken by hook and line except when they approach the shallows and the rivers to spawn, and seldom is one seen during the warm months of the year because of the deeps they frequent. Only in midwinter can their strange primordial mating be observed.

The river mouth was a mile away, opening like a lighted hallway into the black embankment of hills to the south. Beyond its far door were the rapids, a place where the frozen highway of the river was still alive and moving over the rocks. We stopped at the mouth and listened, and there was the same murmuring we had heard the first night we slept on the point, a murmuring that seemed to blend with our breathing and with the pounding of our hearts.

The eelpout need shallow water, moving water full of oxygen, gravel and sand to mix the sperm with the eggs, to keep them rolling over and over until the first cell divisions take place. As we skied up the narrowing river, its sound became plainer until there was a distinct and steady rushing. The rocky shores drew together until they seemed to merge and become part of the woods. Then before us the rapids were suddenly loud and clear and we saw the glint of them in the moonlight. We stopped, unstrapped our skis and went into the trees, stayed quiet until the cold made us move. No vibration of the bank, no breaking twigs must announce our coming. Not until we were within ten feet of the rapids did we shine our lights and then saw such a sight as is seldom glimpsed by modern man, a struggling squirming mass of fish, the brownish snake-like bodies with their sinuous dorsal fins the full length of them twisted around each other, the entire contorted mass turning over and over, churning the water into froth.

Fascinated and oblivious of the cold, we stood and watched, for this was a scene out of the dim past, this mating, the rapids white with the concentration of eggs and milt and the foam from the threshing fish. Over and over rolled the mass, churning the precious eggs and sperms with the liveness of their bodies, whipping them together so there was no chance of an egg not meeting its exploring mate. Out of the depths they had come, swimming into the river and beneath the ice to reach this stretch of open water in the rapids and here in the night exchanging their offerings.

But why in February when the elements seemed against the success of any mating? Why not during the warm days of spring or in the summer or fall when all other species spawned? Why this terrible urge to leave the deeps in the dead of winter and spawn at night? Why does the whiskey-jack lay its eggs during the winter and hatch its young during the bitter days of March? Why does the horned owl do the same? Why do some species violate all traditional procedure? Such thoughts ran through my mind as we stood there and watched the eelpout spawn.

To answer, one must go back to the beginnings of time and find out why these creatures obey urges that today seem beyond reason, urges that were implanted in their genetic structure long before they came to present environments. In the case of the eelpout, a relative of the salt-water cod, it may have been that eons ago it was trapped in the north when the sea that brought it in finally retreated. Perhaps it came in the arm of the sea that laid down the iron deposits of the Mesabi, perhaps from one of the great extensions of glacial waters from the north. Whatever the cause of its introduction, somehow the species managed to survive, adapted itself gradually to the lack of salinity and the shallower depths of inland lakes, changed its habits of feeding and migration; instead of spawning on the ocean reefs it once frequented, it found it could survive by using open streams and the shallows of the lakes. It still keeps the ancient schedule, however, and spawns when the cod spawns in the sea, adhering that much to the age-old habits of the race.

The fish gradually became quiet and the brown eel-like shapes slipped away into the calmer waters below the riffle. There we could see them lying in the shadows, fanning the water with their long finned tails, waiting lazily until the strange apparitions and the unwelcome lights should go away. This was a vital task that brooked no interruption. It was far more important than feeding or any other activity. As with all species, the entire life history led up to this supreme event. It was the climax of existence, the ultimate biological experience toward which everything previous was merely a preparation. When the crucial time was at hand, nothing must ever interfere for long. Like the trout, the salmon, and the eel, these fish had come from the depths to spawn where they themselves had first known the quickening of life. Each year for untold centuries the eelpout had come out of the lake to this particular place and at this very time. Each female left up to half a million or more of some of the smallest eggs produced by fish of inland waters. No wonder the rapids were colored by their release.

The turbulence had ceased and the fish lay furtively in the pool below. We had stopped them in the midst of their ritual, but they would begin again as soon as we were gone. A few nights more and they would swim back into the depths to wait another year before the urge took hold of them again. It was bitterly cold and we had been there for most of an hour. We dropped the flashlights into the pack, strapped on the skis, and pushed back on our trail to the open lake.

While hurrying across the moonlit ice, I could not erase from my mind what we had seen, something that might have taken place in a pool millions of years before. Here was life obeying the urge to reproduce, disregarding all else, bent only on fulfilling the ever implacable law of procreation. For sheer primeval savagery, nothing I had ever seen compared to this. It seemed unreal as the river mouth grew dim behind us and the point ahead lay white and frosty under the moon. I felt somewhat uneasy, as though I had witnessed something I wasn't supposed to see, as though for a guilty moment I had peeked under the curtain at sheer brutality stripped of any of the beauty and joy and delight that is associated with the mating of the animals and birds I knew. Somehow it was as though I had done the unpardonable, stolen a look far back into the dim beginnings of life when forms on earth today were still eons from their origins.

C Test   The Spawning
Finishing Time   _____
WPM   _____

1   The mating of the eelpout takes place in the

   a. spring.

   b. summer.

   c. fall.

   d. winter.

2   The eelpout lay their eggs in

   a. the inland arms of the sea.

   b. lake deeps.

   c. shallow, rushing water.

   d. river bottoms.

3   The fact that the eelpout spawn successfully in midwinter is an example of

   a. adaptation.

   b. regression.

   c. ontogeny.

   d. mitosis.

4   The eelpout churn the water with their bodies

   a. as part of the courtship ritual.

    b. to make a nest for the fertilized eggs.

    c. to stir the water so that the eggs and sperm will meet.

    d. for an unknown reason.

5   The author's reaction to the mating habits of eelpout can best be described as one of

    a. scientific detachment.

    b. fascination and awe.

    c. curiosity.

    d. boredom.

CS = Total number correct _____ × 20 =   %

Speed Test
Starting Time _____

THE SIAMESE TWINS

The Siamese Twins were the most temperamental of Barnum's freak family. Nature had played more than one cruel joke on them. For though Chang and Eng were sentenced to each other, they were opposite in every way and disliked one another. Chang, the slightly shorter one on the Twins' own left, enjoyed wine and women; Eng, the more studious and intellectual, liked an evening of chess. Their differences were reported by the *Philadelphia Medical Times* in 1874: "What Chang liked to eat, Eng detested. Eng was very good-natured, Chang cross and irritable. The sickness of one had no effect upon the other so that while one would be suffering from fever, the pulse of the other would beat at its natural rate. Chang drank pretty heavily—at times getting drunk; but Eng never felt any influence from the debauch of the brother. They often quarrelled; and, of course, under the circumstances their quarrels were bitter. They sometimes came to blows, and on one occasion came under the jurisdiction of the courts."

Left alone, they would brood in silence. Sometimes, they would agree to do first what one wanted, then what the other wanted. Their only interests in common were fishing, hunting, and woodcutting. Although their abnormality had made them wealthy, they lived only to be free of one another. Countless doctors were visited, but not one promised them that they could live a single day cut apart.

Once, after a particularly bitter quarrel, they decided to defy medical advice. According to the *Medical Times:* "Chang and Eng applied to Dr. Hollingsworth to separate them; Eng affirmed that Chang was so bad that he could live no longer with him; and Chang stated that he was satisfied to be separated, only asking that he be given an equal chance with his brother, and that the band be cut exactly in the middle. Cooler counsels prevailed."

Enjoying American freedom and American dollars, the Twins agreed to apply for citizenship. At the naturalization office they learned that they must have a Christian or family name. They had no names other than Chang and Eng. An applicant standing in line behind them, overhearing the nature of the problem, offered his last name. It was Bunker. And so the Siamese Twins became Chang Bunker and Eng Bunker, American citizens.

At last, wearying of the grueling Museum routine, they gave Barnum notice and retired to a plantation near Mount Airy, North Carolina. They relaxed and let their slaves do the work. Then, almost simultaneously, when they were forty-two, they fell in love with the young daughters of a poor Irish farmer in the neighborhood. It was a double wedding. Eng married Sally Yates, and Chang married Addie Yates. Now diplomacy and compromise were required. The Twins built a second mansion, a mile away from the first. Two separate households were established. Chang and Eng and Sally spent three days in Eng's house, and then, Chang and Eng and Addie spent three days in Chang's house. Apparently the arrangement was not inhibiting. The Twins produced twenty-one children.

The Civil War took their slaves and their wealth from them. They were forced back into show business. They asked Barnum to manage them, and he agreed. When their comeback proved unsuccessful in New York, Barnum decided to send them abroad. "I sent them to Great Britain where, in all the principal places, and for about a year, their levees were continually crowded," the showman wrote. "In all probability the great success attending this enterprise was much enhanced, if not actually caused, by extensive announcements in advance that the main purpose of Chang-Eng's visit to Europe was to consult the most eminent medical and surgical talent with regard to the safety of separating the twins."

Again they were wealthy. And again they took leave of Barnum and retired with their wives to the plantation near Mount Airy. They were sixty-three years old, and though Chang had been unwell, the future was bright. The end came suddenly, and the *Annual Register* reported it in 1874. . . .

RECONSTRUCTING THE PAST

Our surest way of reconstructing the past is through looking at the historical record—through looking at the documents, at the fossils, that have survived. Unfortunately, the
record is extremely incomplete, composed of a small and
haphazard collection of fragments, sometimes difficult to
date and always difficult to interpret. We have teeth, jaw
fragments, skulls, sometimes fairly complete skeletons, from
various kinds of manlike animals that have lived at different
places and at different times during the last million years.
And we have a wide variety of tools, mostly of stone, chipped
or polished to shape them for some particular purpose, from
many parts of the world. But how do we put flesh on these
bones? How, from a chipped flint, do we deduce a way
of life?

The fossils, whether bones from the body or tools from
the culture, are clues which must be interpreted. Someone
has suggested that archeologists study police manuals because
the problem of the detective and the problem of the archeologist is the same. Nature has no more intention of leaving
a record than the criminal does and the surviving evidence
is purely the consequence of chance. The evidence is necessarily circumstantial, since we have no eyewitness and no
possibility of finding one. We have only the faint and inade-
quate clues. But these are facts which must be accounted
for, must be explained. The clues serve as take-off points
for our reconstructions, and this is where we have to fall
back on our knowledge of various kinds of living things, on
our knowledge of the behavior of living animals and of the
characteristics of surviving human cultures. In themselves,
these things do not form a historical sequence, but they may
give us, a bit here and a bit there, the evidence needed
for building a possible historical sequence.

The problem of explaining the development of man is
the problem of explaining the development of the human

brain and all the things related to this brain—learning, thought, language, social behavior, culture. As I remarked before, if you look at human anatomy or physiology there doesn't seem to be anything very peculiar about it; but if you look at human behavior, at what men do, it seems to be very peculiar indeed. Man is quite different from anything else in nature, and we have to face the question of how this difference can be explained by natural processes.

Many people—many scientists—have felt that man cannot be explained by natural processes and have fallen back on the supernatural. This seems to me no help at all, since the operation of special supernatural agencies to explain man creates more problems than it solves. If nature is orderly, it ought to be orderly all the way through and I can't see what is gained by supposing some special, miraculous upset in the order back about the middle of Pleistocene times.

It is interesting, in this connection, to look at the difference in opinion between Charles Darwin and Alfred Russel Wallace. Wallace hit upon the idea of evolution through natural selection quite independently of Darwin and the idea was first presented to the world in papers written jointly and read before the Linnean Society on June 30, 1858—a momentous date in the history of ideas.

Darwin, for the rest of his life, felt that the theory served to explain the whole living world, including man and his institutions and ideas. Wallace, perhaps an equally great naturalist, but with a much deeper knowledge of primitive peoples, came to feel that the human mind could not be explained by natural selection or by any other evolutionary process. Wallace thought that the gap between the animal brain and the human brain was so wide that it could not be bridged by imaginable transitions. I don't know of any biologist or anthropologist today who would agree with Wallace; yet, as Loren Eiseley has pointed out in *Darwin's Century*, Wallace in many ways had a more modern understanding of the nature of man than Darwin did.

At that time, the only human fossils that had been discovered were some Neanderthal remains, and these were not recognized as fossil remains of an extinct human type. The evidence for human evolution, then, was entirely comparative, based on the similarities between apes and men. For Darwin, the various savage tribes represented an evolutionary sequence of sorts between the ape condition and the condition of civilized man. Wallace, with his years of travel and living with primitive tribes in South America and Malaya, felt that these people were no different from him in mental ability, moral sense, language development, physical capability, or anything else except material goods—except what we today would call culture. For Wallace, the mind of man was essentially the same everywhere, among all peoples. The Dyak, had he been born in England, might have made a brilliant record at Oxford; while the Englishman, had he been born in the hills of Borneo, would inevitably have followed the Dyak way of life. How could one explain this human mind, with all of its wonderful potentialities, in terms of slow development through selective forces operating in a tropical forest? What, in this environment, would lead to the development of an animal capable of making and running a steam engine or of composing a symphony? It is understandable that Wallace retreated into mysticism.

The difficulty, I think, lies in looking at tools, at culture, as the product of the human brain. For me, the difficulty disappears if we turn the proposition around and look at the human brain as a product, a consequence, of the use of tools, the development of culture. And this sequence is increasingly supported by the accumulating bits of evidence from the fossil record. Some animal has been using tools, shaping rocks, for a very long time, because such stones turn up commonly in deposits that can be dated back to the beginning of the Pleistocene, about a million years ago. And, looking back over the record of this million years, one can see a gradual increase in the skill with which the stones were shaped, and a gradual increase in the diversity of kinds of tools that were made. Improvement and diversity come with increasing speed in the last fifty thousand years, merging into the dizzy rate of change observable in the five thousand years or so of conventional human history.

We have many more fossil tools than we have fossil bones of men or manlike animals, and we only rarely find tools and bones in close association, so that it is difficult to be sure what kind of animal made what kind of tool. Increasingly, however, anthropologists are coming to believe that man in the strict sense, *Homo sapiens,* may be a quite recent evolutionary product, with a history extending back no more than, say, fifty or a hundred thousand years. Most of the Pleistocene tools, then, were made by pre-*sapiens* animals. In the case of Pekin man, *Sinanthropus*—a pretty low-browed fellow—crude stone tools have been found in association with the skeletons.

The greatest interest attaches to the Australopithecines, the South African ape-men, because they represent a very primitive manlike form living about the beginning of the Pleistocene. Did they have fire and did they make tools? The evidence is indirect. These animals did have greatly reduced canine teeth, as do all of the human line, in contrast with the great apes. It can be plausibly argued that the canine teeth would not become reduced in size except in a tool-using animal, which would no longer have need for the big canines.

If we imagine an animal without much more intelligence than, say, a chimpanzee, coming to depend on tools— on sticks and clubs and rocks—we can see that the whole action of natural selection would change. The individuals with the greatest ability to make, and use, tools would be favored. To understand man at all we have to presume, at this beginning of humanness, a social animal with some taste for meat, built in such a way that the hands could be used for handling tools. A cooperating social group with tools could afford to develop—or retain—man's puny physique and generally unspecialized body characteristics. Evolution would turn, not on brawn, but on brains.

It seems that for a long time the chief enemies of men have been men: the force of natural selection has depended on competition within the human or pre-human groups. These socialized, tool-using animals must fairly soon have become relatively safe from the attacks of lions, crocodiles and similar predators. But they also fairly soon took to killing each other on a scale that has no parallel elsewhere in the animal kingdom. If you examine the known human or pre-human fossils with an eye to determining the cause of death, it turns out in a surprisingly large number of cases that the individual, quite clearly, has been murdered. Surviving skulls show that they were pierced by spears or bashed by clubs. Long bones often are split open. No animal except man would be able to split a bone, and the only conceivable purpose in splitting a bone would be to get at the tasty marrow.   This, then, shows that both murder and cannibalism were ancient human practices.

I can understand this only in terms of territorial behavior.   Fighting over territory is common among many kinds of vertebrates.   The loser is rarely, if ever killed; he is simply driven off.   Konrad Lorenz explains this in terms of biological evolution: that as weapons like teeth and claws developed that would enable an individual to kill another member of his own species, inhibiting behavior developed that prevented fighting from being carried to the killing point.   With man, however, weapons are the product of cultural, rather than biological, evolution, and inhibiting behavior has simply not kept pace with weapon development.   But whatever the evolutionary explanation, the result is clear; men have been killing each other for a long time.

If we look at Carpenter's howler monkeys, with their strong clan and territory organization, we can see how this might have developed.   The monkey clans, when they meet on their territorial borders, simply howl at each other until one group or the other retreats.   Monkeys not belonging to the clan are clearly strangers, outsiders, viewed with great suspicion.   The howling is harmless enough; but if these monkeys had spears and clubs, the result of the border squabbles might be quite different.   With primitive, food-gathering people today, we can see a clan and territory organization quite similar to that of Carpenter's monkeys.   And inter-tribal squabbling quite often has deadly consequences.   In cannibalism, the stranger from some foreign tribe is clearly not regarded as human, as a member of the group; and if you kill him, you might as well eat him.   There is no point in letting good meat go to waste, especially when it is so hard to come by.   Which makes humans pretty "inhuman" and "unnatural."

Given this sort of situation, survival and successful reproduction would come to depend on improved ability to make and use tools, and on improved cohesiveness and communication within the effective group—tribe, clan, or whatever you want to call it.   We would thus have continuing selective pressure for what we look at as the distinctively human characteristics.   The individuals and tribes making the most effective weapons and using them most cleverly would win out.   This, at first, would involve biological traits: brain, muscular coordination, speech development and behavioral patterns leading to group solidarity. It would also put a premium on learning, on ability to modify behavior according to the circumstances.

With the development of speech and the possibility of accumulating information (and misinformation), this same intra-human, inter-tribal, competition would guide the development of cultural evolution. From the record of fossil bones and surviving tools, it looks as though once man the animal reached the point of effectively developing cultural traditions, cultural evolution, with its more rapid pace, took over, until now it is the major force governing human characteristics and differences.

But it was a long time before biological evolution was swamped by cultural evolution. The low-browed pre-humans that started using tools were under constant selective pressure to develop the biological equipment—brains, easy upright posture giving freedom to the hands, instinctive and anatomical traits allowing speech development—necessary for the mastery of the tools. Which is why it seems to me that the human brain is more easily understood as a consequence of culture, of tool-using, than as something that had to be developed before culture could be acquired.

But this biological equipment, way back in the Stone Age, reached the point that allowed all of man's subsequent cultural developments to take place. The skills that were required for survival under Stone Age conditions were, it turned out, the skills behind all of man's subsequent bizarre achievement. This is what Darwin failed to understand because he never clearly saw the difference between man as a biological animal and man as a consequence of cultural history. Wallace saw that modern man, biologically, was the same everywhere, and that his differences in accomplishment were the products of his differing cultures, but he failed to see how this potentiality for cultural development could have arisen as a consequence of organic evolution—hence his retreat into mysticism.

Finishing Time _____
WPM _____

PETS . . . OR PESTS?

Most people who acquire a household pet would be hard put to tell you exactly why they did. An animal is brought into the home by a friend, as a gift to a child perhaps, or as a companion for an invalid. Other animals, notably purebred dogs and horses, are kept for enjoyment only, for today they have little use as guardians or as a means of transportation. Cats, once the most useful of small domestic animals in their role of rodent killers, in our times have little work to do, yet remain among the pet world's most desired and ornamental companions.

A pet is a presence. Any living thing accepted as an antidote for loneliness, as an occupation for a child, or a distraction for an older person, will change the emotional climate of the place into which it is brought, or where it is allowed to stay if it happened in by chance.

We may optimistically assume that the change will be for the better, after the period of first adjustment, and that the family scene will be pervaded by affectionate concern for the visitor. Children (we hope) will learn to love their pets, take care of them, and in this new relationship learn to bear responsibility.

Sometimes, when the honeymoon between Junior and his new pet is over, the older members of the household find themselves carrying the load of care and feeding. Burden or not, the pet usually stays on, even to multiply. Save in truly antipathetic households, the elimination of a pet is considered a disaster of sorts, or at least a corollary of disaster. The average family in the Western world, be it rich or quite poor, is a pushover for any new pet that can survive a short trial period and thus establish its right to the affection and attention awaiting it.

. . .

Mankind's tentative and fumbling relationship to the animal kingdom is nowhere better summarized than in its attempt to establish with individual animals a connection which is symbolic and emotionally rewarding for the person, though meaningless for the chosen pet. To be sure, man alone among the animals is concerned with making his gestures meaningful. To live as a pet, for an animal, is simply to have imposed upon its instinctual behavior a group of rules and requirements which must be met without comprehension. Better or worse than what the beast might have encountered in a state of nature, in a life of total risk and relative liberty, no creature will ever assess the difference, for neither regret nor reflection on the comparative aspects of what is past and gone are among its attributes.

People are, by a long shot, the craziest animals. This truth has impressed itself on scientists, philosophers, and self-taught naturalists. If pet animals realized it as well, there would be a prison break of such spectacular proportions that hardly a cage, pen, or poodle pillow would have an occupant. But they don't; more and more live on in a state of strict dependence on the emotional condition of their owners.

Most Americans tender their pets a warm and outgoing love, all the stronger for being aimed at a target that is uncritical. The beloved animal reflects back whatever fantasy his master projects. Even to bite the hand that feeds him is forgiven, as indeed it should be, for it means that something has gone wrong which is no fault of the animal's. What stands as the best protection the pet has against pain, hunger, and thirst is the uniquely human feeling of guilt, which leads its owner to show it consideration and to refrain from all but the most unavoidable violences.

Those who are incapable of love, or who can boast of freedom from guilt feelings at all times, should not have pets. The guilt feelings, to benefit the pet, should manifest themselves whenever a breach occurs in the established routine for the feeding and care of the animal. Conversely, the observance of the routine will in itself tend to keep the owner's anxiety, and whatever lies behind it, under control.

This is by way of saying that if you are an average sort of person (American and European understood to limit the debate), a pet can do a lot for you. What you can do for the pet is another matter. But you certainly can try, and unless the cards are stacked against you, there is a good chance you can keep one pet or more, healthy and tranquil, as a source of pleasure to you and with no great trouble to them.

One way to have the cards stacked against you is to acquire a pet whose chances of survival are poor from the start, and whose brief sojourn in your household will cause, particularly to children, more grief and trouble than pleasure. Included in this list, along with the obviously sick or maimed animals that should be sheltered only long enough to get them into the hands of a veterinarian, are "Easter bunnies," amusement-park chameleons, hand-painted turtles, "Easter" baby chicks and ducks.

The tradition of giving a live animal as an Easter present to a child undoubtedly has the most ancient of origins, but the symbolism has by now become a little confused. In Germany, children are told that if they are good, a white hare will come into their house on Easter eve and hide colored eggs. (In America, the eggs have by extension become live chicks and ducklings, and the hare has become a rabbit.) The hare is a symbol of the moon, for it, too, is nocturnal and has a gestation period of a month. Easter is a holiday fixed by the phases of the moon. Both hare and moon are thought to change their sex, and to be ever open-eyed. New moons are masculine, waning moons are feminine. Baby hares are born with their eyes open, though the rabbit's eyes are closed. Persians believed the world itself was hatched from an egg at the time of the vernal equinox, but they were not the only culture to see in the egg the symbol of the universe and the handwork of divinity. The coloring of the Easter eggs was first done only in red, to symbolize the blood Christ shed on the cross. Finally, the Germanic goddess Ostara, who gave her name to Easter, had a rabbit as her companion.

However rich the jumbled symbolism of the Easter bunny, chick, and duckling may be, there is a relic of barbarism in their eventual fate. Without doubt, most animals sold this way are culls, considered unsuitable for being raised to maturity under the usual conditions. If you can avoid having these poor creatures enter your house and can confine the family's Easter business to the simpler rituals of egg-coloring, egg-rolling, egg-hunting, and the like, you and your children will be the gainers.

Finishing Time _____
WPM _____

Answer Key
for
S&C Selections

Chapter 4

Pretest A. A Nuclear Submarine
1. C   3. B   5. D
2. A   4. A

Pretest B. The Mad Dash
1. C   5. A   8. D
2. D   6. C   9. D
3. A   7. B   10. A
4. B

Pretest C. A View of the United States
1. D   3. A   5. B
2. D   4. C

Chapter 5

Spelman College
1. A   3. C   5. B
2. B   4. D

Training a Dog
1. C   4. A   6. D
2. B   5. B   7. C
3. C

Chapter 6

Sea
1. C   4. C   7. A
2. A   5. B   8. D
3. D   6. D

Wild Rice
1. A   3. B   5. A
2. C   4. B   6. D

The Big Brain
1. B   5. D   8. C
2. C   6. C   9. B
3. B   7. A   10. D
4. A

The Urgency of Lunch
1. B   3. A   5. A
2. D   4. D

Chapter 7

The English Longbow
1. A   3. D   5. C
2. B   4. D

Freud
1. C   4. A   6. A
2. B   5. D   7. D
3. C

Paleolithic Man
1. D   4. D   6. B
2. A   5. B   7. D
3. C

The Coming Crisis in Education
1. D   3. B   5. A
2. D   4. C   6. B

Appendix A

The Tragic Chase
1. D   3. A   5. D
2. B   4. C

Beaver Cutting
1. D   3. C
2. A   4. C

The Spawning
1. D   3. A   5. B
2. C   4. C

TABLE 1. Reading Speed. Number of Words per Minute (WPM) for Selections in the Textbook

Find the column headed with the number of minutes it took you to read the selection. Find the row labeled with the name of the selection. The figure listed where the row and column meet is your reading speed (WPM).

	\multicolumn{9}{c}{Number of Minutes}
	1	1½	2	2½	3	3½	4	4½	5
Chapter 4									
A Nuclear Submarine	1,071	714	536	428	357	306	268	238	214
The Mad Dash	3,271	2,181	1,636	1,308	1,090	935	818	727	654
A View of the United States	1,507	1,005	754	603	502	431	377	335	301
Chapter 5									
Spelman College	1,232	821	616	493	411	352	308	274	246
Training a Dog	1,415	943	708	566	472	404	354	314	283
The Sauna	2,071	1,381	1,036	828	690	592	518	460	414
Chapter 6									
Sea	2,983	1,989	1,492	1,193	994	852	746	663	597
Wild Rice	2,892	1,928	1,446	1,157	964	826	723	643	578
The Big Brain	2,003	1,335	1,002	801	668	572	501	445	401
Urgency of Lunch	956	637	478	382	319	273	239	212	191
A Short History of Surfing	1,055	703	528	422	352	301	264	234	211
Chapter 7									
The English Longbow	712	475	356	285	237	203	178	158	142
Freud	1,060	707	530	424	353	303	265	236	212
Paleolithic Man	2,028	1,352	1,014	811	676	579	507	451	406
The Coming Crisis in Education	1,560	1,040	780	624	520	446	390	347	312
Anthropology as Science and Scholarship	1,155	770	578	462	385	330	289	257	231
Appendix A									
The Tragic Chase	1,690	1,127	845	676	563	483	422	376	338
Beaver Cutting	858	572	429	343	286	245	214	191	172
The Siamese Twins	716	477	358	286	239	204	179	159	143
The Spawning	1,318	879	659	527	439	376	330	293	264
Reconstructing the Past	2,264	1,509	1,132	906	755	647	566	503	453
Pets . . . or Pests?	1,067	711	534	427	356	305	267	237	213

to Read Selection

5½	6	6½	7	7½	8	8½	9	9½	10	10½	11	11½	12
195	178	165	153	143	134	126	119	113	107	102	97	93	89
595	545	503	467	436	409	385	363	344	327	312	297	284	272
274	251	232	215	201	188	177	167	159	151	144	137	131	126
224	205	190	176	164	154	145	137	130	123	117	112	107	103
257	236	218	202	189	177	166	157	149	142	135	129	123	118
376	345	319	296	276	259	244	230	218	207	197	188	180	172
542	497	459	426	398	373	351	331	314	298	284	271	259	248
526	482	445	413	386	362	340	321	304	289	275	263	251	241
364	334	308	286	267	250	236	222	211	200	191	182	174	167
174	159	147	136	127	120	112	106	101	96	91	87	83	80
192	176	162	151	141	132	124	117	111	106	100	96	92	88
129	119	110	102	95	89	84	79	75	71	68	65	62	59
193	177	163	151	141	132	125	118	112	106	101	96	92	88
369	338	312	290	270	254	238	225	213	203	193	184	176	169
284	260	240	223	208	195	184	173	164	156	148	142	136	130
210	192	178	165	154	144	136	128	122	116	110	105	100	96
307	282	260	241	225	211	199	188	178	169	161	154	147	141
156	143	132	122	114	107	101	95	90	86	82	78	75	72
130	119	110	102	95	90	84	80	75	72	68	65	62	60
240	220	203	188	176	165	155	146	139	132	126	120	115	110
412	377	348	323	302	283	266	252	238	226	216	206	197	189
194	178	164	152	142	133	126	118	112	107	102	97	93	89

198

a guide to rapid reading

TABLE 2. Reading Speed. Number of Words per Minute (WPM) for Passages That Are 300 to 1,600 Words Long

Find the column headed with the number of minutes it took you to read the passage. Find the row labeled with the number of words in the passage you read. The figure listed where the row and column meet is your reading speed (WPM).

Number of Words in Passage	Number of Minutes to Read Passage									
	½	1	1½	2	2½	3	3½	4	4½	5
300	600	300	200	150	120	100	86	75	67	60
350	700	350	233	175	140	117	100	88	78	70
400	800	400	267	200	160	133	114	100	89	80
450	900	450	300	225	180	150	128	112	100	90
500	1,000	500	333	250	200	167	143	125	111	100
550	1,100	550	367	275	220	183	157	138	122	110
600	1,200	600	400	300	240	200	171	150	133	120
650	1,300	650	433	325	260	217	186	162	144	130
700	1,400	700	467	350	280	233	200	175	156	140
750	1,500	750	500	375	300	250	214	188	167	150
800	1,600	800	533	400	320	267	228	200	178	160
850	1,700	850	567	425	340	283	243	212	189	170
900	1,800	900	600	450	360	300	257	225	200	180
950	1,900	950	633	475	380	317	271	238	211	190
1,000	2,000	1,000	667	500	400	333	286	250	222	200
1,050	2,100	1,050	700	525	420	350	300	262	233	210
1,100	2,200	1,100	733	550	440	367	314	275	244	220
1,150	2,300	1,150	767	575	460	383	328	288	256	230
1,200	2,400	1,200	800	600	480	400	343	300	267	240
1,250	2,500	1,250	833	625	500	417	357	312	278	250
1,300	2,600	1,300	867	650	520	433	371	325	289	260
1,350	2,700	1,350	900	675	540	450	386	338	300	270
1,400	2,800	1,400	933	700	560	467	400	350	311	280
1,450	2,900	1,450	967	725	580	483	414	362	322	290
1,500	3,000	1,500	1,000	750	600	500	428	375	333	300
1,550	3,100	1,550	1,033	775	620	517	443	388	344	310
1,600	3,200	1,600	1,067	800	640	533	457	400	356	320

Chart 1. Record of Reading Speed (WPM) on Selections in the Textbook

| Selection | Reading Speed (WPM) |

Chapter 4
A Nuclear Submarine
The Mad Dash
A View of the United States

Chapter 5
Spelman College
Training a Dog
The Sauna

Chapter 6
Sea
Wild Rice
The Big Brain
The Urgency of Lunch
A Short History of Surfing

Chapter 7
The English Longbow
Freud
Paleolithic Man
The Coming Crisis in Education
Anthropology as Science and Scholarship

Appendix A
The Tragic Chase
Beaver Cutting
The Siamese Twins
The Spawning
Reconstructing the Past
Pets . . . or Pests?

200

a guide to rapid reading

Chart 2. Record of Reading Comprehension (CS) on Selections in the Textbook

Selection   Comprehension Score (CS)

Chapter 4
A Nuclear Submarine
The Mad Dash
A View of the United States

Chapter 5
Spelman College
Training a Dog

Chapter 6
Sea
Wild Rice
The Big Brain
The Urgency of Lunch

Chapter 7
The English Longbow
Freud
Paleolithic Man
The Coming Crisis in Education

Appendix A
The Tragic Chase
Beaver Cutting
The Spawning

Chart 3. Record of Reading Speed (WPM) in Practice Books and Outside Reading

Source of Selection   Reading Speed (WPM)